VOTING BEHAVIOUR

and

ELECTORAL SYSTEMS

Chris Robinson

Series Editor: David Simpson

Hodder & Stoughton

A MEMBER OF THE HODDER HEADLINE GROUP

ACKNOWLEDGEMENTS

The publishers would like to thank the following for granting permission to reproduce pictures in this book:

BBC: page 43
The Sun and Remember When: page 54
The Associated Press: pages 95 and 106

Order queries: please contact Bookpoint Ltd, 39 Milton Park, Abingdon, Oxon OX14 4TD. Telephone: (44) 01235 400414, Fax: (44) 01235 400454. Lines are open from 9.00–6.00, Monday to Saturday, with a 24 hour message answering service. Email address: orders@bookpoint.co.uk

A catalogue record for this title is available from The British Library

ISBN 0 340 711353

First published 1998
Impression number 10   9   8   7   6   5   4   3
Year   2004   2003   2002   2001   2000

Copyright © 1998, Chris Robinson

Cover illustration by Martin Haswell.

Typeset by Transet Limited, Coventry, England.
Printed in Great Britain for Hodder & Stoughton Educational, a division of Hodder Headline plc, 338 Euston Road, London NW1 3BH by Redwood Books, Trowbridge, Wilts.

CONTENTS

PREFACE

A/AS Level syllabuses in Government and Politics aim to develop knowledge and understanding of the political system of the UK. They cover its local, national and European Union dimensions, and include comparative studies of aspects of other political systems, in order to ensure an understanding of the distinctive nature of the British political system. The minimum requirements for comparative study are aspects of systems with a separation of powers, how other systems protect the rights of individuals and how other electoral systems work.

Access to Politics is a series of concise topic books which cover the syllabus requirements, providing students with the necessary resources to complete the course successfully.

General advice on approaching exam questions

To achieve high grades you need to demonstrate consistency. Clearly address all parts of a question, make good use of essay plans or notes, and plan your time to cover all the questions.

Make your answers stand out from the crowd by using contemporary material to illustrate them. You should read a quality newspaper and listen to or watch appropriate programmes on radio and television.

Skills Advice

You should comprehend, synthesise and interpret political information in a variety of forms:

- Analyse and evaluate political institutions, processes and behaviour, political arguments and explanations.
- Identify parallels, connections, similarities and differences between aspects of the political systems studied.
- Select and organise relevant material to construct arguments and explanations leading to reasoned conclusions.
- Communicate the arguments with relevance, clarity and coherence, using vocabulary appropriate to the study of Government and Politics.

David Simpson

1

INTRODUCTION

THIS BOOK COVERS two, seemingly disparate topics. The first theme is voting behaviour: the patterns and trends in **psephology** over the past 40 years. The second theme is electoral systems: the workings of both the British system and those of other countries. The use of the word 'seemingly' is deliberate. Despite the fact that, hitherto, one would expect to see the two bodies of subject matter covered separately, they both have a direct bearing on one another.

The first-past-the-post voting system has been criticised for decades. Indeed, between the First and Second World Wars, a number of attempts were made to change it. Interestingly, this was also a period of political realignment, with the Liberal Party being replaced as the second major party and the Conservatives taking advantage of the split opposition. In the first two decades after the end of the Second World War, Labour and the Conservatives jointly presided over a political system where up to 97 per cent of the voters supported them. The issue of electoral reform, therefore, was not on the agenda, save for the odd **by-election** upset in the late 1950s and early 1960s. It was true that even at the height of the **two-party system**, neither Labour nor the Conservatives could muster 50 per cent of the vote in office, but it seemed that most people did not think too much about it.

Over the past 15 years, however, much has been written about the changing nature of voting behaviour in Britain. The stability and the certainties that were its major characteristics a generation ago now seem to have been replaced by instabilities and uncertainties, and this in spite of 18 continuous years of Conservative rule. Governments can be elected with 100-seat majorities and yet poll fewer votes than the previous election when they only had a majority of 20. Political parties may be within two percentage points of one another, but one might have 10 times more seats than the other. Political parties may pick up 15 per cent of the national vote and yet win no seats in an election for the European Parliament.

Such are the anomalies of the electoral system today. The inadequacies of the system have to some extent been exposed by the changes in voting behaviour over the past 40 years. These inadequacies have always been there, although their practical manifestations did not catch the public mood in the way that seems to be the case today. One does not wish to ascribe a causal relationship between the changes in voting behaviour and the calls for electoral reform, as many of the latter's strongest adherents would claim that that is opportunistic – and that their cause is one to be judged on its own merits. Nonetheless, the situation remains that were it not for some of the glaring anomalies that are now so apparent in the British electoral system, perhaps the calls for its overhaul would not be quite so loud.

The volume of these calls has at last received a sympathetic hearing in government, a number of whose most senior ministers are adherent of change. Mr Blair 'remains unconvinced', but there are clear signals that changes are on the way. Early in 1999, legislation passed through Parliament, which resulted in **proportional representation** in elections to the European Parliament in 1999. Legislation has already been passed to include proportional elements to the systems used to elect members of the Scottish Parliament and the Welsh Assembly. The Prime Minister also asked the former Labour Home Secretary (and former leader of the SDP), Lord Jenkins of Hillhead, to investigate alternative voting systems for elections to Westminster.

This book will first examine the manner in which voting behaviour has changed over the past 40 years, and discover whether this has helped raise the saliency of electoral reform. It will then examine alternative types of voting system, with brief case studies about countries where these systems operate.

THE STUDY OF ELECTIONS AND VOTING BEHAVIOUR

This is a very important element of A and AS Level syllabuses, and is also a key part of many undergraduate degree courses. This book should be able to assist those who are studying voting behaviour and different electoral systems. This is particularly the case given the increasing emphasis being given to the teaching of comparative politics as part of the core syllabus at GCE. The following themes are central to questions which might arise on the topics contained in this book:

- The main characteristics of voting in Britain since the 1950s. Can any trends be discerned?
- The main forces which appear to shape public opinion and help form the support for the political parties.
- How has the mass media influenced opinion and voting behaviour? What are the changing trends in this respect?
- To what extent have changes in voting behaviour added impetus to the calls for changing the electoral system?

- What are the key features of the main alternatives to the first-past-the-post system?
- What are the relative merits of these systems?
- What are the consequences of these systems in the countries in which they are used?

The questions which appear at the end of each chapter are designed to help explore these themes as well as to suggest ways that examination questions may appear. As a general point, it is important to recognise the key words that appear in questions. Many focus on the idea of 'change', which effectively means it is not enough to make lists of functions and characteristics without mentioning the dynamics of the situation. Look out for key words such as this, for they literally are the ways to unlock a question and to provide a good, strong and relevant answer.

2

ELECTORAL TRENDS IN THE 1950s AND 1960s

Introduction

THIS CHAPTER WILL look at the voting behaviour in Britain during the 1950s and 1960s. It will offer evidence showing why this era has been characterised as a 'two party' period of political stability. It will also look at various measures of party popularity, as well as alternative analyses of this period.

Key points
- The evidence for a two-party system.
- Other party-popularity measures.
- Alternative insights.

A TWO-PARTY SYSTEM

British politics in the 1950s and the 1960s has often been characterised by a number of descriptions. The era has been described as being 'two party' in nature, a period of political stability with voting behaviour being firmly anchored by a number of social alignments (of which more in the following chapter).

Examining the electoral statistics of the time, one can understand why these conclusions were reached. This is even clearer after the events of the 1970s, 1980s and 1990s. The chart shown on page 5 gives a flavour of the levels of political support in British general elections during those years. There would appear to be some support for the label 'two party'. The chart amply demonstrates that this

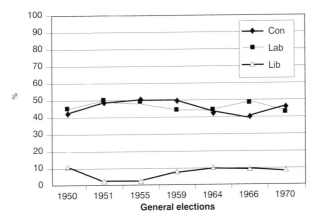

FIGURE 1: PARTY SUPPORT IN BRITISH GENERAL ELECTIONS 1950–1970
SOURCE: BUTLER AND BUTLER, 1994 PP 216–17.

was so. The nearest third party (the Liberals) languished in single percentage support for virtually the whole period, while Labour and the Conservatives enjoyed support never falling below 40 per cent of the electorate each. The stability of this two-party dominance has been the subject of much study, and some explanations of the phenomenon are offered in the next chapter.

If one were to aggregate the support of the Conservative and Labour parties, the scale of their dominance would become apparent. The pie chart shown below offers a stunning picture of this dominance averaged out over the 20 years between 1950 and 1970.

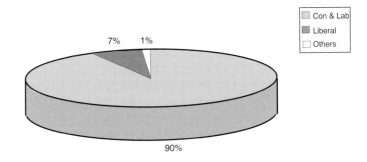

FIGURE 2: AVERAGE PERCENTAGE VOTE IN BRITISH GENERAL ELECTIONS 1950–1970
SOURCE: ADAPTED FROM ELECTION DATA IN BUTLER AND BUTLER, 1994.

THIRD-PARTY UNDERREPRESENTATION

The sheer dominance of votes commanded by the two main political parties meant that in the 1950s in particular, third parties were a virtual irrelevance. It is difficult to see how the issue of electoral reform could be expected to be the subject of popular debate. Indeed, it was a topic which was largely confined to academic circles, with the Liberal Party in particular being unable to gain a wider currency in the form of general awareness of the issue.

It remains true that third parties were underrepresented in the House of Commons at this time, but compared with the period after 1974, this was far less significant. The two graphs shown below indicate the disparity which existed between votes and seats at general elections between 1950 and 1970 for the

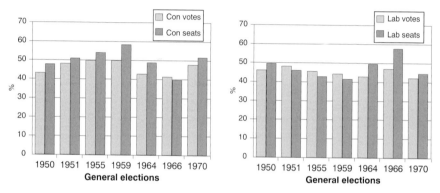

FIGURE 3: CONSERVATIVE AND LABOUR SHARES OF VOTES AND SEATS IN BRITISH GENERAL ELECTIONS, 1950–1970
SOURCE: ADAPTED FROM ELECTION DATA IN BUTLER AND BUTLER, 1994, PP 216–217.

Conservative and Labour parties. As may be seen from these graphs, there is a disparity between the seats gained by each of the main parties and the number of votes obtained. In each case, the disparity was large enough to maintain a government with a Parliamentary majority without a majority of votes. This in itself is a criticism of the electoral system during the period (through it was nothing like as serious as trends noted in Chapter 4). More worrying perhaps is the chronic underrepresentation of the Liberal Party at this time, which although nothing like as bad as it was in the 1970s, still left hundreds of thousands of voters without a voice in Parliament. The graph shown in Figure 4 illustrates this point. This chart has a different scale which in some ways tends to overestimate the degree of the disparity. Nonetheless, the relative difference between Liberal votes and seats is much greater than is the case for either the Labour Party or the Conservative Party. This said, in absolute terms, the numbers of voters actually supporting the Liberals during this period was small, and therefore the unfairness of the system hardly gained popular attention at the time.

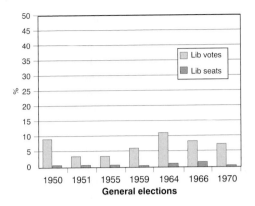

FIGURE 4: LIBERAL SHARE OF VOTES IN BRITISH GENERAL ELECTIONS, 1950–1970
SOURCE: ADAPTED FROM ELECTION DATA IN BUTLER AND BUTLER, 1994, PP 216–17.

Even in the 1950s and 1960s, the British electoral system could be accused of harming smaller parties, although it is probably more accurate to say that it merely emphasised the dominance of the Conservative and Labour parties. In Parliamentary terms, this domination was almost complete. There were few Members of Parliament not taking the Conservative or Labour whip.

The bar graph in Figure 5 shows the extent to which the two main parties dominated the House of Commons during this period. It is almost impossible to see the seats occupied by Liberals and others because there were so few of them. During this period the combined share of the seats held by Conservative and Labour MPs never fell below 97 per cent.

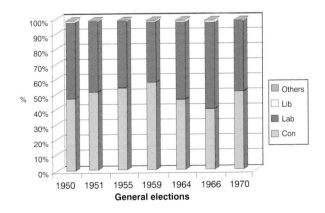

FIGURE 5: PERCENTAGE SHARE OF HOUSE OF COMMONS SEATS, 1950–1970
SOURCE: ADAPTED FROM ELECTION DATA IN BUTLER AND BUTLER, 1994, PP 216–17.

OTHER PARTY-POPULARITY MEASURES

There are other measures of party political popularity that may be examined. The most notable are opinion-poll findings and the results of by-elections – see the graph below. It must be admitted at this point that these pieces of evidence present a more ambiguous picture. In neither case do they show the overwhelming two-party support found in Figures 1 and 5. However, they do show very impressive levels of support which nowadays political parties might envy.

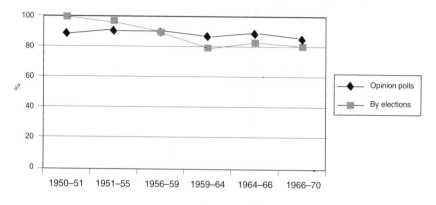

<small>Figure 6: Conservative and Labour share of polls and by-elections, 1950–1970
Source: adapted from Norris, 1997, p 39.</small>

It may be noted that the figures for both polls and by-elections are relatively high, and that level of two-party support in polls is far more consistent over the period. The figures for by-elections are somewhat mixed, however. During the 1950s, Labour and the Conservatives fare particularly well. In the 1960s, however, there is a marked drop in support for the two. This may have been somewhat portentous for the decades ahead where by-election victories for third parties ceased to be a political novelty.

ALTERNATIVE INSIGHTS

At this point, some attention needs to be given to alternative analysis of this period. Some writers have attempted to reinterpret the nature of the party system in the 1950s and 1960s. Richard Rose offered numerous indicators to question whether the system was two-party in nature during this time. Andrew Heywood prefers to see the period as one of dominant party (the Conservatives), with the period between 1964 and 1979 then somewhat aberrant. Between 1951 and 1964 and between 1979 and 1997, the British political system was dominated by the Conservatives.

These arguments provide useful alternative insights which remind us that a blind acceptance of the two-party description requires some qualification. However, this cannot deny the evidence which points towards that description as being accurate for the time. Indeed, between 1945 and 1979, both Labour and the Conservatives occupied the same time (approximately 17 years) in government. As indicated in Figures 1 and 5, voting at general elections (and in particular the ones with the greatest level of participation) strongly indicated a two-party system, and other indicative factors such as opinion polls and, to a lesser degree, by-elections all reinforce this appraisal.

What is impressive in the above analysis is the political stability that existed during this period. This can be seen by the first chart in Figure 7 which shows how little both political parties deviated from a statistical mean over the period. This compares with the situation which prevailed after 1970, a foretaste of which is outlined in the second of the charts covering the years between 1970 and 1997.

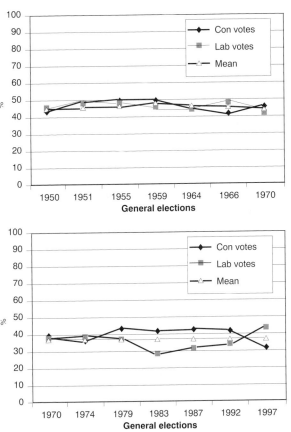

FIGURE 7: TWO-PARTY DEVIATION FROM THE MEAN, 1950–1970 AND 1970–1997
SOURCE: ADAPTED FROM ELECTION DATA IN BUTLER AND BUTLER, 1994.

The question which should be asked at this point is why Britain possessed such a stable, two-party political system during this period. The following chapter seeks to offer an explanation of why up to 97 per cent of voters were willing to put their trust in the Labour and Conservative parties for nearly a generation.

SUMMARY

The label 'two-party' has been attributed to the period between 1950 and 1970.

The period was also characterised by a marked degree of electoral stability.

The Conservative and Labour parties commanded all but a handful of seats in the House of Commons.

This Parliamentary strength was based upon an overwhelming two-party share of the popular vote.

Other measures of political support, such as opinion-poll ratings and by-election results, confirmed the dominance of the Conservative and Labour parties.

The position of the Liberal Party in the 1950 was almost terminal, with as few as three in a hundred voters supporting them. Apart from the occasional by-election victory, the party never made significant inroads into the popular vote.

Although the Liberals were underrepresented in the House of Commons at the time, the issue of electoral reform never reached the main political agenda.

STUDY GUIDES

Revision Hints

You do not have to possess a detailed knowledge of this period. Rather, you should understand this era as setting the context for what was to follow in later decades.

The changing fortunes of the political parties from the 1970s onwards may be put into sharp relief against this period, displaying two-party dominance.

When revising different types of party system, this period provides good statistical data relating to two-party systems.

Do not ignore the position of third parties. The term 'main parties' usually means the Liberals as well as Labour and the Conservatives.

Remember that there are some serious challenges to the two-party thesis. You should be familiar with the objections to it in broad terms.

Exam Hints

- Examine the various ways in which two-party dominance may be measured.
- Examine the role of third parties during this period. How does it compare with the situation today?
- What are the main reasons why some commentators reject the idea of a two-party system?

Practice Questions

1 How accurate is the term 'two-party' when describing the British political system in the 1950s and 1960s?

2 How significant was the debate on electoral reform in the two decades up to 1970?

3 'The Liberals were a political irrelevance in the 1950s and 1960s.' Discuss.

3

EXPLAINING VOTING BEHAVIOUR 1950–1970

Introduction

THIS CHAPTER WILL consider several theories of voting behaviour. It will first discuss rational voter theory, and explain why this is not an adequate approach. It will then go on to look in detail both at class alignment and at partisan alignment, explaining why these are the two most important determinants of voting behaviour.

Key points

- Rational voter theory.
- Class alignment.
- Partisan alignment.

The previous chapter outlined the nature of the political system in the two decades until 1970. The picture was one of two parties dominating the political scene. Why was it that during this time voters seemed so loyal to just two political parties?

What makes people vote the way they do? Many explanations have been suggested for voter choice. Some have revolved around factors such as party leaders, candidate personality or even the appearance of the politician. In the run-up to the 1983 General Election, the Labour leader Michael Foot came in for frequent press criticism for his somewhat unorthodox dress sense (on Remembrance Sunday in 1981, he was reported to be wearing a donkey jacket at the official ceremony at the Cenotaph in Whitehall). Before the 1997 General Election, a survey of women voters showed a dislike for Tony Blair's hairstyle.

Clearly, a myriad of factors might affect individuals differently. What is important, however, is to examine the way individuals behave in groups. Much of the research taking place into the study of voting behaviour is based on the responses of real voters in surveys and questionnaires. Many of the issues raised in this and subsequent chapters are based on the findings from this type of research.

RATIONAL VOTER THEORY

Nowadays, it is expected that scholarly output in this subject be based upon quantitative research methods. This has not always been the case. Books written about voting behaviour before the 1950s tended to stress very traditional, some might say almost mythical, conceptions of the voter. These largely emphasised the *rational* nature of the voting. This theory stressed the role of the voter as that of carefully weighing up the arguments over a range of issues before finally choosing a candidate or party. The meaning of the word 'issues' here has long been subject to debate. Butler and Stokes offer the following distinction between:

> '... *issues that are defined in terms of alternative courses of government action and issues that are defined in terms of goals and values that government may achieve,*'

Concluding

> '... *It is natural that the analysis of issues should have a bias towards issues that have meaning in terms of alternative policies.*'

Butler and Stokes, 1974.

Modern cynics of this view may argue that endowing the voter with a high degree of rationality might in some way have offset the impact of a very centralised and hierarchical political structure which in reality gave (and to some degree still gives) most voters very limited influence.

This assessment of voter choice was not confined solely to Britain. Writers in the USA in the early part of this century also conferred on voters this rational status. The result of this approach was that for decades, very little research was conducted on voting behaviour, and where major issues were discussed, the focus was judgmental rather than analytical. Viscount Bryce, writing shortly after the end of the First World War, described such a rational voter:

> *The man of broad common sense, mixing on equal terms with his neighbours, forming a fair and unprejudiced judgement on every question*

Viscount Bryce, *Modern Democracies*, London, 1921, pp 168–169.

REASSESSING RATIONAL VOTER THEORY

If early theories about voting behaviour could be placed within a general 'classical' theory based more on traditionally cherished notions of the workings of the British Constitution than on critical observation, then the period since the 1950s would be characterised by a more scientific and empirical approach. A new breed of experts emerged, and their 'science' was psephology.

The difficulty with rational voter theory is that it bore little truth to what was really happening. Research in the 1950s and 1960s in both Britain and the USA found a major contradiction between voters' positions on issues and their party support. Successive opinion polls throughout the postwar period showed an **ideological disjuncture** between Labour supporters and the Party itself on issues such as capital punishment for example.

In the USA, the seminal work by Campbell *et al.* attempted to explode the myth of the rational voter, offering in its place a model of voting behaviour which seemed better equipped to explain voter choice. On the question of voters carefully evaluating issues, they concluded:

Many people fail to appreciate that an issue exists, others are insufficiently involved to pay attention recognised issues, and still others fail to make connections between issue positions and party policy

Campbell, Converse, Miller and Stokes, 1960, p. 183.

Furthermore, it has been found that over time, attitudes were far from consistently held, with voters changing their minds on issues in significant numbers. Butler and Stokes found that a number of key issues there was a major lack of consistency expressed. Surveys carried out using the same respondents in the early to mid-1960s showed a far-from-impressive level of consistency of opinions on issues such as nationalisation and Europe, leading the authors to conclude:

It seems more plausible to interpret the fluidity of the public's views as an indication of the limited degree to which attitudes are formed towards even the best-known of policy issues

Butler and Stokes, 1974, p 281.

The conclusions of Campbell *et al.* and Butler and Stokes may not come as much of a surprise to some contemporary observers, but two factors should be borne in mind. Much of what has been claimed in rational voter theory implies a knowledge and evaluation of issues as the basis of party choice. The texts *The American Voter* and, latterly, *Political Change in Britain* seriously question the impact of issues, and indeed show that opinions on issues were highly volatile among those interviewed in surveys. The latter point is crucial, since in the 1950s and 1960s, voting behaviour remained very stable, as Table 1 illustrates. In four of the elections over this period, over half the constituencies had a **swing** which was within 1 per cent of the national average. This relatively consistent behaviour and stability of political support contrasts sharply with the volatility of attitudes to issues discussed earlier.

Table 1: *Percentage swings between Conservative and Labour in British general elections, 1950–1966*	
GENERAL ELECTION	PERCENTAGE SWING
1950	2.9 to Con
1951	1.1 to Con
1955	1.8 to Con
1959	1.1 to Con
1964	3.1 to Lab
1966	2.7 to Lab

SOURCE: PULZER, 1975, P 100.

ALTERNATIVE EXPLANATIONS OF VOTING BEHAVIOUR

How could the apparent contradiction of relatively stable voting patterns and issue volatility be reconciled? If one wishes to stick to rational voter theory, the answer is simple: they can not. Other theories need to be examined. The studies of Campbell *et al.* In the USA and of Butler and Stokes in Britain, were the works which would attempt to provide alternative explanations. David Denver creates a useful synthesis of much of this research. Of the 1950s and 1960s, he writes:

> *Broadly speaking, the electorate was divided into two large blocs which provided reliable and stable voting support for the Conservative and Labour parties. The interconnected phenomena of class and partisan alignment were the twin pillars … which supported and sustained stable party support on the part of individual voters and a stable two-party system overall.*

Denver, 1994, pp 31–2.

CLASS ALIGNMENT

Research in the 1950s and 1960s in both Britain and the USA showed that of all the factors which might determine a person's voting behaviour (including gender, age, religion and regional locality), **social class** was by far the most accurate predictor. Put crudely, in Britain at this time, working-class people tended to vote Labour, while those from the middle class were overwhelmingly Conservative Party supporters.

The question of what actually constitutes class has long been fraught with difficulties. Should one's class be determined by income? If so, then at this time a coal miner, docker or steelworker would be middle class, given the more modest earnings of most office workers, many administrators and civil servants, who by implication would be working class. An added complication is that of so-called *self-assigned class* where individuals perceive themselves as being in a particular social class without any objective justification for the claim.

A measure of social class

Mercifully, over the past 90 years, a measurement of social class has emerged which has become acceptable to both academic and commercial communities alike. This measurement is based upon occupation, and although it has been subject to some modification (and, it must be said, to more recent challenge), it remains the most widely used measure of social class.

Most polling organisations, whether acting on behalf of the BBC, a national newspaper or a soap-powder manufacturer, will base their research on one of a number of occupational measurements. The most frequently used measurement offers the following breakdown:

- A   Higher Professional, Managerial & Administrative
- B   Intermediate Professional, Managerial & Administrative
- C1 Supervisory Clerical & Other Non-Manual
- C2 Skilled Manual
- D   Semi & Unskilled Manual
- E   Residual & Casual Workers. People on State Benefit

(Based on the social classification of the Registrar General's Office.)

It is usual to speak in broad terms about social class, using the middle-class/working-class dichotomy. The middle class may be defined in terms of the three non-manual categories of the above list (grades ABC1). The working class may be identified by the manual groups (grades C2DE). During the 1950s and 1960s, there appeared to be a close correlation between social class and support for political parties – see the graph on page 17.

At this point, it should be noted that there is not a perfect match between social class and party support. Indeed, if one looks at the figures for the manual, working class during the period covered by the table, between a quarter and a third voted Conservative. The number of middle-class Labour supporters is more modest, but at between a fifth and a quarter during the period, it is far from insignificant. These **deviant voters** may be explained in a number of ways.

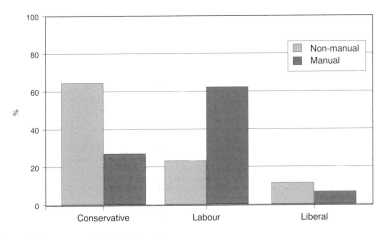

FIGURE 8: CLASS VOTING 1959–1970
SOURCE: ADAPTED FROM BUTLER AND STOKES, 1974

Explaining deviant voting

Middle-class supporters of the Labour Party were traditionally to be found in the professions rather than in business. Teachers, lecturers and doctors all had significant levels of support for Labour. This may be compared to managers in the business community who were overwhelmingly Conservative in nature. Working-class Conservatives were a crucial element of the two-party equation in the postwar years. Given that the working class amounted for two-thirds of the voting population in the 1950s and 1960s, a party which was able to command all of this vote would have found itself in a permanent state of government. The presence of significant levels of working-class support, however, meant that throughout this period, the Conservative and Labour parties had roughly a half each of the popular support of the country. As such, the working-class Conservative has been of greater political significance, and therefore of academic interest as well. Peter Pulzer offers the following observation:

---

the Conservative Party has survived the democratization of the country by its ability to gain votes from the poor. For that reason the Tory working-man has been subjected to more study than the middle-class Socialist. While some middle-class sympathy may be important to the Labour Party in providing it with leadership and local organization, and perhaps also in confirming its claim to speak to the workers 'by hand and by brain', it does not have the statistical significance that the working-class support has for the Conservatives.

Pulzer, 1975, p 109.

How may one account for the phenomenon of the working-class Conservative? For the period under discussion, there are a number of explanations. The major one concerns the notion of *social deference*, where individuals perceive Conservative politicians as their betters and therefore suited to being leaders of the country.

The Conservatives have had more experience over the centuries. It's in the blood for them, running the country. There's more family background in the Conservatives, more of the aristocratic families, more heritage.

They're gentlemen born. I think they're made for that sort of job

R. Samuel, 'The deference voter' in *New Left Review*, Vol. 1, January–February 1960, p 11.

There are a number of alternative explanations of working-class Conservatism, however, including the impact of **cross-class location**, where the membership of the working class is complicated by factors such as home ownership, or where the voters place themselves in the wrong social class. Detailed analysis of this phenomenon is really beyond the scope of this book. (See the Denver (1994), McKenzie and Silver (1968) and Nordlinger (1967) references in the 'Further Reading' section at the end of this book).

Within these limitations, it remained the case that of all the possible influences that could affect voting behaviour, social class was by far the most influential. Indeed, in 1967, Peter Pulzer's well-worn quotation-cum-academic-sound-bite summarised the position at the time rather well:

Class is the basis of British party politics; all else is embellishment and detail

Pulzer, 1975, p 98.

If class was the basis of British party politics at this time, what was the basis for class-voting? As can be seen from the first reference in this chapter to the work of Butler and Stokes, rational evalution of issues does not appear to be the explanation. Indeed, given that these researchers witnessed significant shifts of opinion from their respondents on important issues, one would have expected a more volatile voting pattern if a widespread, rational connection had been made between opinions on issues and votes.

It would seem more likely that class-based voting was rooted in a more general perception about which party was most likely to defend the interests of certain groups with which individuals identified, rather than in careful evaluation of specific issues. Put crudely, the Labour Party was seen by the majority of the working class as the party most likely to look after it in such areas as employment and welfare. Conversely, the middle class shared the broad Conservative beliefs

in social hierarchy, defence of traditional values and the importance of the creation and conservation of wealth. Furthermore, the middle class felt hostility to the Labour Party, in that it was perceived that Labour would somehow 'hurt' its class interests.

Butler and Stokes, in some open questioning, were able to glean the thoughts behind the votes, and they did indeed paint a picture of a generalised belief system rather than a well-developed appreciation of issues. The following is a collection of quotations gleaned through the open questioning of survey respondents:

(Likes about Labour 1963) *'More for the working class. They believe in helping those who need it – like old people and people with large families'*

(Likes about Labour 1966) *'They are better for the working-class. They do more for us. They have a better idea of what does us most good and they understand our problems better'*

(Dislikes about Labour 1963) *'This attitude about money. They seem to think they can rob the rich to save the poor'*

(Dislikes about Labour 1966) *'I don't like their attitude towards the richer people – that they are the ones who should pay for all the extras and help that the poor people get'*

Butler and Stokes, 1974, pp 84–85.

Class and voting: a conclusion

So far, it has been suggested that in the 1950s and 1960s, voters did not behave rationally when it came to party choice. A number of factors were of importance in influencing voting behaviour, and social class emerged as the most significant. There was strong loyalty among members of the working class for the Labour Party, with the overwhelming majority of middle-class voters supporting the Conservatives. This tendency was not rock solid, however: a significant number of working-class voters supported the Conservatives.

This notwithstanding, voting behaviour heavily influenced by social class was a well-established and accepted theory by the 1970s. It was not the only explanation, however. Another alignment based upon the idea of **partisan alignment** or **party identification** was also crucial to our understanding of the influences on voting behaviour.

PARTISAN ALIGNMENT

Partisan alignment was first established as an important phenomenon in helping explain voting behaviour in the 1950s. The authors of *The American Voter* described it as follows:

> *A psychological attachment to party, varying in direction and intensity*
>
> Campbell, Converse, Miller and Stokes, 1960.

What this means is that voters do not simply vote for a political party on a momentary whim but instead hold an enduring bond with a political party (in the case of the USA, either Democrat or Republican). This bond could be strong, moderately strong or weak. The stronger the party identification, the stronger the bond, and consequently the more durable a voter's loyalty to a party. Butler and Stokes, when conducting their own research of the phenomenon in Britain, found that during this time, levels of party identification were high and that indeed:

> *in 1963 well over four-fifths of our respondents said they had always supported the same party*
>
> Butler and Stokes, 1974, p 40.

Although the authors regarded this figure as a probable exaggeration, it indicated a great level of stability from one election to another in those days. Voters more readily accepted the labels 'Labour', 'Conservative' and 'Liberal' being attached to them: people did not simply vote Conservative, they saw themselves *as* Conservatives, for example. Indeed, the standard question to establish the presence and nature of party identification, used in the Butler and Stokes surveys at the time, was as follows:

> *Generally speaking do you usually think of yourself as Conservative, Labour, a Liberal or what?*
>
> Butler and Stokes, 1974, Appendix B, p 470.

During this period, voters overwhelmingly accepted one of these options. Table 2 demonstrates this very clearly.

Table 2: *Level of party identification 1964–1970*			
	1964	1966	1970
% with party identification	93	91	90
% identifying with Con	38	35	40
% identifying with Lab	43	46	42

SOURCE: ADAPTED FROM CREWE, IN DENVER AND HANDS, 1992, CHAPTER 4. 2, P 143.

Throughout the 1960s, nine out of ten voters identified with one of the political parties, and to support the evidence of the previous chapter, eight out of ten identified with either Labour or the Conservatives. As was briefly mentioned earlier, it was not just the level of party identification that was noted: the strength of partisanship was also observed – see Table 3.

Table 3: *Strength of party identification 1964–1970*			
	1964	1966	1970
% very strong identifiers	44	44	42
% fairly strong identifiers	38	38	37
% not very strong identifiers	11	9	11
non-identifiers	7	9	10

SOURCE: ADAPTED FROM CREWE, IN DENVER AND HANDS, 1992, CHAPTER 4. 2, P 143.

By adding together the very strong and fairly strong identifiers, it may be seen that during the 1960s, consistently more than 80 per cent of the electorate had at least a fairly strong attachment to their chosen political party. The figures may be further refined by concentrating attention on those who identified very strongly with the Conservative and Labour parties – see Table 4.

Table 4: *Strength of Conservative and Labour identification 1964–1970*			
	1964	1966	1970
% very strong Conservative and Labour identifiers	40	39	40

SOURCE: ADAPTED FROM SARLVIK AND CREWE, 1983, PP 334–5.

A stabilising factor

Clearly, the strength of partisanship during this time helps explain the stable, two-party system during the 1960s characterised in the previous chapter. **Recall data** collected by Butler and Stokes from the time of the 1959 General Election offers findings consistent with the notion that strong partisanship was a major force shaping electoral behaviour during the 1950s and 1960s. The electorate displayed great loyalty to their chosen party at this time, the strength of which appears to have been decisive in maintaining consistency in voting behaviour. Even when an individual did change their vote, it was often the case that they maintained their identification with their original party. In other words, party identification tended to endure even when party support in elections changed.

This phenomenon of identification endurance should not be overstated, however. Butler and Stokes did stress that this was of far greater significance in the US presidential elections at the time than it was in Britain. It did, however, remain a noticeable phenomenon. The graph below shows the ebbs and flows of both the party identification ('partisan self-image') and the vote of the Labour Party during the 1960s.

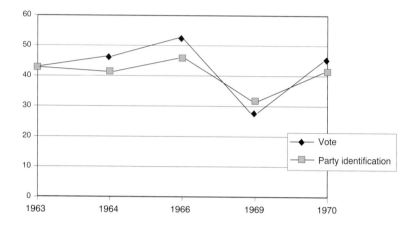

FIGURE 9: LABOUR'S SHARE OF PARTISAN SELF-IMAGES AND VOTE PREFERENCE, 1963–1970
SOURCE: BUTLER AND STOKES, 1974. P 45.

It is important therefore to stress once more that party identification conveys something more than just the simple act of registering support for a political party at election time. It many be seen almost as a psychological anchor which moors a voter's allegiance to a political party, even when that party may be enduring a 'storm'. The result, as the previous chapter illustrates, is an era where the main parties are able to hold on to the bulk of their supporters even during or after very difficult times.

This chapter has concentrated on two very important determinants of voting behaviour during the 1960s and 1970s. It would be very misleading to say that these factors affected such behaviour uniformly across Britain. Electoral behaviour in Northern Ireland did not follow similar trends to those in Great Britain. Indeed, religious factors appear to have been (and remain) important in determining the support for political parties in Ulster. Religion is one of a number of factors which have often been seen as determinants of voting behaviour in Britain. Other factors include regional location, and age and gender. Once again, study into these areas goes beyond the remit of this book. A number of publications offer in-depth analysis (Butler and Stokes, 1974) or a more general (and therefore more appropriate for this level of study) approach (Denver, 1994).

The main forces at work during this period were those of social class and party identification. Together, these forces complemented one another in maintaining a political system dominated by the Conservative and Labour parties. It seemed that a new political mould was cast in this era, and there seemed little on the surface to cast shadows over a political two-party elite content in the knowledge that it had respective loyal followings to maintain strong Parliamentary presences even in electoral defeat.

SUMMARY

Rationality is not an adequate way to explain voter choice during this period.

Evidence suggests that voters could not accurately identify party stances on particular issues.

Great shifts in attitudes were measured at a time when party support remained comparatively stable.

Two phenomena, social class and partisan self-image, appeared to be the anchors which maintained the stability of the political system in Britain at this time.

Working-class people tended to vote Labour, while middle-class people were overwhelmingly likely to support the Conservatives.

This was not a hard and fast rule, however. There were deviants, that is voters who did not support their natural party of class.

Party identification is a psychological attachment to a political party. It was not simply voting for a party, it was a feeling almost of belonging to a party (not to be confused with party membership of course).

During this period, an average of 90 per cent of voters identified with one of the main political parties, while 80 per cent were fairly or very strongly attached.

STUDY GUIDES

Revision Hints

Once again, the focus of this chapter is on the context. The idea is to provide an understanding of why voters behaved the way they did in the 1950s and 1960s. It is unlikely that a thorough knowledge of these explanations will be required.

There are some key concepts with which you should be familiar; you should understand the terms 'partisan alignment' and 'class alignment' as key factors affecting political support.

Remember to understand the period on its merits. Do not confuse issues which may be important today with ones which were of little significance a generation ago (for example, newspapers would appear to have a greater influence in Britain in the 1990s than they did 30 or 40 years ago).

Exam Hints

- Some of the shorter quotes are useful to learn (Pulzer's on the influence of class, used in this chapter). The use of quotations shows an examiner that you have read around the subject and that the ideas you are putting forward have been researched.
- Do not try to remember great swathes of statistics. Pick up key figures, and average out lists so that there is a judicious use of numbers. This will not only display a grasp of the topic but also enable an essay or other response to flow more smoothly. An examiner will hence find it easier to read.
- Remember to define social class in precise terms: it is classification based on occupation.
- When looking at the impact of social class, remember that a significant (and in the case of the working-class, crucial) proportion of individuals does not support its 'natural party of class'.
- Partisan alignment is not the same as voting or political support. It is enduring and entrenched, psychologically, in the minds of individuals.

Practice Questions

1 How important were issues, during this time, in determining voter choice?
2 What factors helped maintain the great alignments of party identification and social class?
3 Apart from social class and party identification, what other factors might have affected voter choice at this time?
4 What is deviant voting? Account for this tendency in the 1950s and 1960s.

4

ELECTORAL TRENDS AFTER 1970

Introduction

THIS CHAPTER WILL look at the increasing volatility in voter behaviour in Britain after 1970, charting increasing attention to the issue of electoral reform, the rise of smaller parties, increasing vote–seat disparities, the rise of the Centre parties, and the dramatic decline and resurgence of the Labour Party.

Key points

- Electoral reform on the agenda.
- The rise of smaller parties.
- Vote–seat disparities.
- The rise of the Centre parties.
- The decline and recovery of Labour.

INCREASING VOLATILITY

'Unstable' and 'volatile' hardly seem appropriate words to use after 18 years of continuous one-party government. However, after the 1970 General Election the certainties of the 1950s and 1960s appeared to evaporate. The February-1974 General Election resulted in the first minority government in Britain since 1929. The February election also saw not only the fall in support for the Heath government but also a corresponding decline in the vote of Wilson's Labour opposition. The smaller political parties claimed that neither Labour nor the Conservatives were able to claim a right to govern Britain, and the success of nationalist parties in Scotland and (to a lesser extent) Wales put further pressure on a political system whose governing party (Labour) was elected to office with nearly a quarter of a million fewer votes than the Conservatives who had lost on seats.

The extent of the change in the fortunes of the political parties is amply demonstrated by Table 5. This outlines the average share of the vote obtained by the major political parties during the four main phases of Conservative and Labour governments from 1951 up until 1979. The columns of the chart denote the periods of government and the corresponding periods of opposition for the two main parties. The period from 1951 to 1964, for example, was a period of Conservative rule and Labour opposition.

Table 5: *Average percentage shares of the vote for Conservative, Labour and Liberal, 1951–1979*				
	1951–1964	1964–1970	1970–1974	1974–1979
Conservative	49.0	42.7	46.4	36.9
Labour	46.0	46.0	43.0	38.2
Liberal	3.7	9.9	7.5	18.8

SOURCE: EXTRACTED FROM BUTLER AND BUTLER, 1994. FIGURES DO NOT INCLUDE THE ELECTION DATA FOR 1979.

In the first three periods, levels of support for the two main parties remained high. The average level of support throughout these years was 46 per cent for the Conservatives and 45 per cent for Labour. The Liberals achieved a very low level during the same period (only 7 per cent). These figures contrast starkly with those for the elections of February and October 1974. The average combined share of the vote for Labour and the Conservatives in the six elections between 1951 and 1970 was 91 per cent. This had declined to just over 75 per cent in 1974. The speed with which this decline took place, however, may be seen by examining the period between 1970 and 1974. As late as 1970, Labour and the Conservatives were able to command a combined vote of 89.4 per cent. This declined by nearly 15 per cent in the following four years.

It had been common to describe the British political system as two-party in nature, and with Labour and the Conservatives able to obtain nine out of every ten votes cast in the 1950s and 1960s, this description appeared to be appropriate. The Liberal Party were virtually an electoral irrelevance in the 1950s, and their average level of support in general elections in the 1960s remained below 10 per cent.

THE QUESTION OF ELECTORAL REFORM

The question of electoral reform was not a significant one during this period. In the 1950s, a proportional result would have added between 10 and 15 seats to the Liberal total. In the 1960s, the Liberals would have earned around 50 extra seats. In other words, the system would have remained, in the main, dominated by Labour and the Conservatives (arch defenders of proportional representation (PR) would no doubt argue that any redistribution, no matter how small, is fairer than a non-proportional system, and it may be argued that Labour would not have achieved a Parliamentary majority in the election of 1964 if PR rules had applied).

The picture in 1974, however, was of a different magnitude. The Liberals had polled just under a fifth of the national vote and could have expected over 100 extra seats from a proportional system. No longer could the overwhelming electoral dominance of the two main political parties be used to dismiss calls for electoral reform. For perhaps the first time since the 1920s, it appeared that the main political players were being propped up by a voting system which was denying a voice to millions of voters and suppressing the representation of other political parties.

THE RISE OF SMALLER PARTIES

This picture, however, is not as simple as so far painted. The elections of 1974 brought not only the Liberals into the forefront of the British political system (for a few days after the result of the February poll, it seemed possible that there could even have been a Conservative-Liberal **coalition government**). Other political forces also stirred at this time, notably the nationalist movement in Scotland. During the 1960s, both the Scottish National Party (SNP) and the Welsh nationalists, Plaid Cymru, had scored notable by-election successes. Plaid Cymru's vote peaked at just over 175,000 votes in the 1970 General Election, and in the elections of 1974 the SNP were able to poll up to 30 per cent of the Scottish vote.

In October 1974, the SNP won 11 seats in the House of Commons, and although polling over 800,000 votes in Scotland, this only represented 2.9 per cent of the vote in Britain as a whole. Compare this with the Liberals, who in 1955 polled just over 700,000 votes, constituting 2.7 per cent of the total, resulting in 6 seats. More seriously, a comparison between the Liberals and the SNP in October 1974 makes sobering reading, as Table 6 illustrates.

It is clear that not all minor political parties suffer from the first-past-the-post electoral system to the same extent. Although the SNP would have been likely to benefit from about extra 8 seats under some form of proportional voting, this is nothing like the extra 100 seats that the Liberals would have won.

Table 6: *Liberal–SNP comparison for the October 1974 General Election*			
Oct–1974 General Election	Seats	% vote	% seats
Liberal	13	18.3	2.0
Scottish National Party	11	2.9	1.7

SOURCE: EXTRACTED FROM BUTLER AND BUTLER, 1994.

A party fielding relatively few candidates, in a nationally and culturally specific region, is likely to be able to amass a relatively modest number of votes per candidate fielded and still win a respectable percentage of the seats it fought. In October 1974, the SNP fought in 70 constituencies (all Scottish), with 11 candidates winning seats, a 16 per-cent success rate. The Liberals fielded 619 candidates but only achieved success in 13 constituencies, only a 2 per-cent success rate.

A political party with popular support very thinly distributed across the country (such as the Liberal Democrats even today) is likely to fare less well than a party with relatively concentrated support, such as nationalist parties like the SNP and, traditionally, to an extent, both Labour and the Conservatives.

The picture is somewhat more complicated when studied more carefully. What is quite clear is that after 1974, the voting public punished both the major parties, the net beneficiaries being the Liberals (at least in terms of votes) and the Scottish Nationalists (in terms of both votes and seats).

As for the two main political parties, their fortunes plummeted in the early 1970s, as may be seen in the bar graph below. As the graph shows, up until the 1960s,

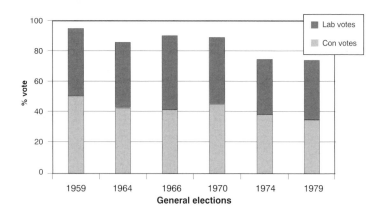

FIGURE 10: COMBINED CONSERVATIVE–LABOUR SHARE OF THE VOTE 1959–1974
SOURCE: ABSTRACTED FROM STATISTICS IN BUTLER AND BUTLER, 1994.

Labour and the Conservatives were able to enjoy combined support of over 90 per cent of the electorate. In 1974, however, this figure fell to 75 per cent. This needs to be seen in the context of what had gone before. Between 1951 and 1970, the combined share had never fallen below 87.5 per cent. In the scope of three and a half years, however, it fell 15 per cent.

It would have been tempting at the time to see this as an aberration, a short-term phenomenon which would go away after the next election. Certainly, after the election in February 1974, Harold Wilson's game plan was to do what he had done in 1964: govern for a short period and then consolidate his position after a year or two. In 1974, however, Wilson did not have the luxury of a year. With only 301 out of 635 House of Commons seats, the second election would come sooner rather than later. In fact, it came in October of the same year.

Far from restoring normality to the political process, the election of October 1974 confirmed what some had feared, that forces more fundamental than first thought were at work. Wilson and his successor James Callaghan struggled through the 1970s, first with a tiny majority and then slumping back into minority, before finally succumbing to the will of Parliament and then the people in the spring of 1979.

FURTHER UNCERTAINTIES

The result of the General election of May 1979 did lead many to believe that the two-party system had clicked back into place. Indeed, the new Conservative government had a healthy majority, and no one questioned their ability to carry on for a full five-year term. The Liberal Party seemed to have peaked, and their support now fell back sharply. The nationalist tide appeared to have turned, and the much-heralded rise of the far Right failed to materialise.

Such assessments were misplaced, however. Far from signifying a return to normality (whatever that may be), the fact of the matter is that the 1979 result was further evidence that the political certainties of a generation were crumbling. The Conservative victory saw the biggest swing of any election since the Second World War. Furthermore, the swing was most prominent among skilled working-class voters, the so-called C2s. It would appear that the **volatility** which resulted in the minority governments of the 1970s was still at work and causing political upheaval.

Certainly, the combined share of the vote for Labour and the Conservatives increased in 1979, but only up to just over 80 per cent, a far cry from a generation before when the figure was up in the 90s. Indeed, if we look at the figures for 1983, 1987, 1992 and even the **landslide** of 1997, it may be seen that at no time does this combined share of the vote rise above 80 per cent. Indeed, for most of this time, it is languishing in the low 70s (lower in fact than in the 1974 elections).

VOTE—SEAT DISPARITIES

Interestingly, by 1979 it becomes possible for a government to secure a healthy Commons majority with just over 40 per cent of the vote, and this contrasts sharply with elections in the 1950s and 1960s. Table 7 offers the comparison.

Table 7: *Government majorities and percentages of votes, 1955–1997*		
ELECTION	GOVT MAJORITY	GOVT % VOTES
1955	58 seats	49.7
1959	100 seats	49.4
1966	96 seats	47.9
1983	144 seats	42.4
1987	102 seats	43.4
1997	160 seats	44.1

SOURCE: ADAPTED FROM BUTLER AND BUTLER, 1994.

In the first series of elections, the winning party commanded just under half the vote, with majorities reaching up to 100 seats. After 1979 (and excluding the 1992 General Election), parties have polled up to 9 per cent less and yet have majorities well over 100. The lack of any seeming relationship between votes and seats has seen majorities rise with the overall level of party support being lower. This is not intended to imply any meaningful correlation, only to indicate that by the last two decades of the twentieth century, our voting system was producing some strange results.

Clearly, some elections have been omitted from this analysis, and these often show a different story. In 1992, the Conservatives were returned to power with just over 43 per cent of the vote but only managed a majority of 21. This underlies the uncertainty of relationship compared to a generation ago. More than this, the system seemed to be producing almost random results.

If the manner in which governing parties were being returned to office had the air of a lottery about it, then the way in which the votes of the opposition parties were translated into seats bordered on the almost farcical.

THE RISE OF THE CENTRE PARTIES

Perhaps the most notorious election of the 1980s was in 1983, with Mrs Thatcher massively increasing her majority and yet seeing her share of the popular vote fall. The focus of this election, however, was not the performance of the Conservative Party but the discrepancies between Labour and the SDP–Liberal Alliance.

The SDP was a party formed, in the main, by disaffected supporters of the Labour Party as it moved leftwards in the years immediately following its election defeat in 1979. Shortly after its formation in the Spring of 1981, the SDP leadership moved to form an electoral pact with the Liberal Party. In 1983, this 'Alliance' was positioned between Labour, with perhaps its most socialist manifesto ever, and the rightwing (but, in the wake of the Falklands War, popular) Thatcher government.

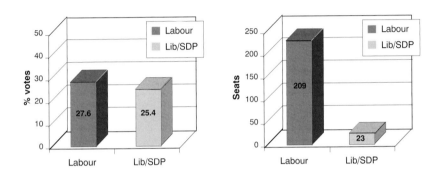

FIGURE 11: LABOUR AND LIBERAL–SDP ALLIANCE VOTES AND SEATS IN THE 1983 GENERAL ELECTION
SOURCE: ABSTRACTED FROM STATISTICS IN BUTLER AND BUTLER, 1994.

The first of the two bar graphs in Figure 11 shows just how close the Liberal–SDP Alliance came to displacing Labour as the second force in British politics. The Labour Party's support had collapsed, and the Alliance was only 2 per cent behind it. The euphoria that the Centre parties might have felt is immediately dampened, however, when one looks at how these votes translated into seats – see the second of the two bar graphs. The Labour Party had very nearly 10 times as many seats as the Alliance, despite being only fractionally ahead in votes.

Two factors are worthy of note here: first, of course, there is the huge disparity between votes and seats which re-ignited the debate for a fairer electoral system; second, and perhaps more significantly, what had happened to the Labour Party? It is true, the result has to be seen in the light of the Labour manifesto – '… the longest suicide note in history' was how Gerald Kaufman described it. But the extent of the fall was surely greater than a manifesto could achieve by itself.

There was the image-of-the-leadership question. Compare Margaret Thatcher moving effortlessly from one photo-opportunity to the next with Michael Foot who, if the cruel, rightwing press were to be believed, had trouble moving at all. However, even the liability of a leader would not have made the party so unpopular.

If this had been the 1950s and not the 1980s, then it is likely that the above observations would again have been true. Indeed, manifestos and leadership qualities were even less likely to have been such devastating factors in those days. After all, in the last chapter we saw just how firm the support was for the political parties, being as it was rooted to social class and partisanship. If Labour had lost the equivalent election in the 1950s, it is doubtful that it would have suffered such a major rout. Indeed, looking at its elections of 1955 and 1959, we see that Labour was able to command 46.4 and 43.8 per cent of the vote respectively (both these figures higher than any government achieved in the 1970s and 1980s).

Another factor that should be noted at this point is about the performance of the Alliance parties. It is unthinkable 30 years before that any party of the Centre could have made the electoral impact that the Liberals and the SDP made in June 1983. David Owen wanted to break the mould of British politics. Maybe he did not break it, but there would appear to have been forces at work which were transforming it.

Two phenomena were developing: the increase in support for third parties; and the decline in support for the Labour Party. At the time, some of the Centre-Left believed that a realignment was taking place with Labour becoming increasingly marginalised and the Centre parties seeking to occupy its vacated position. This view was perhaps understandable but nonetheless premature. A realignment would assume a movement from one settled position to another. There was little evidence that this was indeed the picture.

A LABOUR GOVERNMENT IN WAITING

In the late 1970s, culminating in the General Election of 1979, a shift in support was noted among skilled working-class voters from Labour to the Conservatives, and the early 1980s, it would appear that yet another group of voters were deserting Labour for the Centre parties. However, this may have constituted a dealignment rather than a realignment of support. There was nothing to suggest that these voters had shifted to permanent new party residences. Indeed, the political earthquake that resulted in Labour's return to power in 1997 underlies this point all too well.

Voters do not behave in a vacuum: they are affected by many factors. Some of these are fundamental and socioeconomic (see the next chapter) while others are most transient and have a greater connection with day-to-day politics. Labour did not continue its slide into oblivion, as many on the Right and in the Centre predicted. The very election result which supposedly marked the beginning of its terminal decline was instead the turning point for the party to start rebuilding its shattered fortunes. Far from spurring on the Centre-party alliance to greater things, the period after 1983 was somewhat moribund for the SDP and the Liberals.

The Conservatives won four successive elections between 1979 and 1992, and two of these returned the government with majorities of over 100 seats. Electoral success, however, did not save Margaret Thatcher from her own Parliamentary party, which turned its back on her in 1990, nervous at opinion-poll ratings and predicting a heavy defeat at the next election. Throughout her period in office, she suffered some of the worst popularity figures in the history of polling, and yet despite this, the party came back to win time and again.

So it was again in 1992, when the Conservatives defied the pundits and won the election of that year. The victory was in many ways a hollow one. The Conservative majority was slashed from 100 down to 21. A series of political and economic setbacks befell the government, and the Cabinet was hopelessly split over the issue of Europe. By contrast, the Labour opposition, for the first time, had the air of a government in waiting. It seemed that the longer the Conservatives kept the voters waiting, the harder they would be punished.

In recounting these last days for the Conservatives, it is important to understand that the forces at work in 1997 were, in part, the same forces at work in 1979 and 1983. Voters who had attached themselves to political parties for a generation were becoming detached, and new voters were not being socialised to support any one political party. In 1979, it was the Conservatives who benefited from this phenomenon. In 1997, however, Labour were the main beneficiaries. Political support had become more volatile, and parties appeared to be more vulnerable to swings in public mood. Those who thought they had found political certainties in the 1980s had to drastically rethink their conclusions after 1 May 1997.

SUMMARY

Between 1970 and 1974, there was a major and rapid fall in support for Labour and the Conservatives. Between 1970 and 1974, the two parties lost 15 per cent of their combined vote to other parties.

Britain saw its first minority government in 45 years.

Electoral reform was on the agenda, with the Liberals obtaining nearly one-fifth of the vote but winning under 2 per cent of seats in the House of Commons.

Not all smaller parties suffered as a result of the electoral system. The SNP won nearly as many seats as the Liberals in October 1974, with a fraction of the votes.

The Conservative victory in 1979 convinced many that the instabilities of the 1970s were only temporary. A close look at the seismic shifts of working-class votes from Labour to the Conservatives would prove otherwise.

Volatility seemed now to be the watchword. There appeared to be no relationship between the size of a government's majority and the size of its vote.

This volatility spilled into the opposition parties. In 1983, Labour came only a couple of per cent ahead of the Liberal–SDP Alliance and yet won 10 times as many seats.

Labour appeared to have been the early victims of these changes, and yet, despite being written off as late as the early 1990s, seemed to have reaped political rewards from there being a volatile electorate.

There would appear to have been no realignment involved, just a crumbling of the old certainties outlined in Chapter 3.

STUDY GUIDES

Revision Hints

The beginning of this period (the early 1970s) is crucial in understanding the changes in postwar electoral behaviour.

The possible reasons for why there was such a sudden change in political support need to be addressed.

Examine the differing electoral performances of third parties at this time (especially compare the Liberals and the Scottish National Party in the early 1970s).

The success of the Conservatives (in the 1980s, in particular) needs to be examined in the context of political shifts first seen in the early 1970s. Does it mark a return to stability, or is it a further manifestation of the breakdown in this stability?

Exam Hints

- Examination questions about constitutional change often focus on the period after 1970.
- The rise of third parties in British politics is a key theme for questions about this period.
- Questions on electoral reform require factual analysis about how the British voting system has proved weak. Examples from specific elections should be used.

- When looking at electoral reform, it is tempting to focus merely on the position of the government vis-à-vis the state of other parties. Remember, however, that disparities exist between different opposition parties as well (for example, the position of Labour and the Liberal–SDP Alliance after the General Election of 1983).

Practice Questions

1 How and why has constitutional reform come onto the political agenda in the last 30 years?
2 Compare and contrast the political fortunes of the Liberals and the Scottish National Party in recent elections.
3 To what extent did Britain acquire a dominant-party system after 1979?
4 In which ways and to what extent has Britain become politically more volatile in recent years?

5

EXPLAINING POLITICAL VOLATILITY AFTER 1970

Introduction

THIS CHAPTER WILL try to explain the cause of increased voter volatility after 1970. It will look at the various reasons first for partisan dealignment, and then for class dealignment, moving on then to a discussion of volatility, and to one redefinition of social class.

Key points

- Reasons for partisan dealignment.
- Reasons for class dealignment.
- Volatility.
- A redefinition of social class.

The previous chapter examined the sudden decline in support for the Conservatives and Labour in the early 1970s and the rise in the fortunes for third parties. It went on to look at the 1980s and 1990s, the dominance of the Conservatives and the seeming decline and then miraculous recovery of the Labour Party. The main thesis of this chapter was that all these conflicting phenomena were in fact the result of the same political and electoral forces.

In Chapter 3, an attempt was made to explain stable, two-party voting by using the concepts of **class alignment** and **partisan alignment**. Political parties were able to weather many a storm and still retain their support largely intact. Of course, parties lost as well as won elections, but the shifts in political support from one to the other (the swings) were never great. The two main parties appeared to take it in turns to run the country. Third parties, who might score the odd success at by-elections, never made inroads into the vote of the two main parties. By the 1970s, this was no longer the result of the system.

If it were not for the first-past-the-post voting system, it is likely that the political shifts of opinion which took place after 1970 would have had a greater and much more immediate impact on government in Britain. As it was, despite losing millions of votes between them, Labour and the Conservatives attempted to go along 'business as usual'.

What were the forces at work which brought about the changes in voting behaviour? Had the old certainties been replaced with anything else as fixed?

In the late 1970s, important research was published which appeared to indicate that weaknesses in the old alignments were taking place. Indeed the origins of these changes went back to when the so-called 'era of alignment' was in full swing (see pages 15-23). 1970 would seem to be a useful date after which the effects of these changes could be seen.

It would appear that in the two key areas of class and partisanship, changes were taking place. The era of alignment, it would seem, had given way to the era of dealignment. In other words, a weakening of party identification and social class as the major influences were taking place. It is possible, therefore, to talk in terms of **partisan dealignment** and **class dealignment**.

PARTISAN DEALIGNMENT

Earlier in this book, we examined the findings of Butler and Stokes which showed that nine out of ten voters identified with a political party and that just over four in ten had very strong attachment to 'their' party. By contrast, in the 1980s and early 1990s, the picture was somewhat different. Voters still tended to identify with a particular party in similar numbers, but the strength of this identification appeared to have weakened significantly. The bar graph shown on page 38 offers a picture of the changes.

The Figures 12 refers to identification for all political parties. The overall and strong identification patterns for Labour and the Conservatives match these trends.

People still seem able to identify themselves with a particular political party. They are unable, however, to commit themselves strongly to one. The figure for strong party identification more than halved over the period being discussed. As it is strong identifiers who are likely to be the more enduring in terms of their willingness to turn out and vote for the same party time after time, we begin to see where problems arise for those parties which benefited most from this phenomenon.

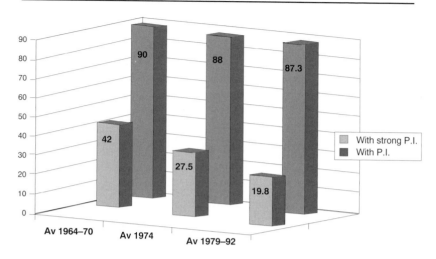

FIGURE 12: PARTY IDENTIFICATION 1964–1992
SOURCE: ADAPTED FROM DENVER, 1994, P 54.

The very core of support for both political parties appears to have shrunk. What is left seems to be a mass of voters who can make the psychological attachment to a party but whose support would appear to be more conditional on a range of other factors. Clearly this will have impact upon parties at election time because a strong identifier is less likely to be swayed by events or crises than a person whose partisanship is weaker. Consequently, the more weaker identifiers there are, the greater potential for other factors to influence them.

REASONS FOR THE WEAKENING OF PARTISANSHIP

Increased voter awareness

Overall, heightened political awareness, combined with (if not responsible for) an electorate increasingly cynical with main political parties, appears to have eroded the strength of party identification over time.

It may be argued that the electorate is more aware of issues and more willing to be affected by them. Following the expansion of the university sector in the early 1960s and the continued growth in higher education since then, there may be a case for suggesting that overall levels of education have affected voter loyalties. Crewe, Sarlvik and Alt (1977) have suggested that in the period of their study (1964–75), it was among those with higher-education qualifications where the greatest decline in the strength of partisanship had taken place.

It may be argued that a more educated electorate is able to weigh up issues in a more objective fashion and is less likely to have formed an emotional relationship with a single political party. If the relationship between voter and a party is more rational, this then might explain the increasingly conditional nature of this relationship. The success or otherwise of a political party may increasingly depend on its ability to deliver when in government.

There is a somewhat worrying aspect to this line of argument, however, as it would appear to suggest that the only people capable of making a sensible judgement at election times are those with more education. This somewhat elitist interpretation has resonances with the views of the nineteenth-century liberal tradition in fearing the rule of the mob. It should be stressed at this point that no attempt is being made to offer value judgements about the changes to the strength of partisanship.

The fact remains that even in the 1970s and 1980s, the increasing population of students in higher education would not be sufficient to explain the major electoral and political changes that were going on at this time. Similarly, there is no guarantee that a person with a degree in quantum mechanics or astrophysics is going to be more capable of voting rationally than someone with a couple of GCSEs in English and Mathematics.

The impact of television

There are other sources of information about politics. Newspapers don't just offer political information, they also offer views and comment as well. To what extent can this influence voters? The impact of newspapers and other media will be examined in the next chapter, but it would be worth mentioning a few words at this point on the significance of television.

Television coverage of politics is a relatively new phenomenon. Indeed, it was not until the General Election of 1959 that there was the sort of coverage that we might recognise today. Even then, the coverage of Richard Dimbleby was far more deferential in tone than we would expect in the 1990s from either of his sons, David or Jonathan. In the 1960s, the likes of Robin Day and David Frost adopted a more interrogatory style and turned the political interview into more of a trial by television.

Politicians could now be seen in more human terms, their weaknesses exposed for millions to see, their policies put under the spotlight and their arguments scrutinised for inconsistencies. Gone were the days when a party leader could effectively determine the conduct and outcome of a television interview, and it could be argued that, over time, this may have had an impact upon the perceptions of the millions watching.

The lack of deference towards our political leaders broadened into popular culture as well. In the early 1960s, the satirical magazine *Private Eye* was launched and has thrived ever since on a diet of lampoon, political gossip and investigative journalism. Television was no stranger to this phenomenon. *That Was The Week That Was* featured many sketches aimed at deflating the importance of the political elite. Since then, the likes of Rory Bremner and the Spitting Image team have provided a picture of politicians with warts and very little else.

No attempt is being made here to quantify the effects of this type of television coverage. It is clear, however, that our politicians are probably taken less at their face value now than they were 40 years ago. This may affect the way in which people's attitudes to politics generally are reflected.

On its own, however, this is probably not enough to decrease partisan strength. For a satirist to be guaranteed a laugh, they must strike a chord with the audience. If politicians were doing everything right, then satirists would probably find themselves out of a job.

Party promises

For the jibes of comics and satirists to ring true, political parties must have been doing something wrong in the first place. Over the past 40 years, our political leaders have been promising to deliver the people from bad times (usually caused by leaders of the opposing parties) to better ones. The history of Britain in the postwar years has usually found governments making bad situations worse.

In some respects, this is the result of a combination of factors. Politicians have spent much of this time promising better times, and voters have come to have increasing expectations of what the politicians can do. In the 1950s, with a growing economy and years of relative prosperity, governments were able to deliver on promises. Hospitals were opened, schools were replaced and council houses were built. By the 1960s, however, this era was over, with the country facing economic problems, such as unemployment, balance-of-payments difficulties and inflation. These problems were often experienced in turn, and occasionally at the same time. Unfortunately, however, the politicians still promised and the voters still expected. it only becomes a matter of time before the electorate realised that neither party in office are delivering what they said they would do in opposition. It perhaps should not be surprising that the voters then become more than a little wary of party promises.

Labour's move to the Centre

The last chapter examined the near-terminal decline of the Labour Party in the early 1980s. It may be seen that Labour has been particularly badly hit during this era of dealignment. Between 1970 and 1997, Labour was in power for just over five years. The Conservatives, by contrast, were in power for 18 consecutive years. Were there forces at work in which were particularly harmful to Labour? Was it these forces with which Labour battled between 1983 and 1997? By shifting its position in key policy areas, was Labour able to turn these forces to its own advantage?

There is evidence to suggest that an increasing number of voters (including Labour ones) were becoming disaffected by traditional socialist policies such as nationalisation and trade union power (Crewe and Denver, 1985) The reasons for this may be inextricably linked with changes in social class (discussed later in this chapter). Clearly, following its electoral defeat in 1983, Labour could have chosen one of two directions in which to travel: first, it could have continued along the road on which it had started out, at the beginning of the 1980s, waiting for the 'inevitable' crisis in capitalism; alternatively, it could begin the journey back to the centre ground in the hope of recapturing its lost support.

Labour chose the latter course, and in so doing, it has been claimed, abandoned everything it stood for. The rights and wrongs of what happened are for a different debate. Clearly, however, in the long term, the party managed to overcome some of the negative stereotypes which some believe kept it out of government for so long.

To conclude this section of the chapter, party identification has weakened, and this has been ascribed to the increasing political awareness/cynicism of the electorate. Labour in particular has had a particularly high mountain to climb (compared with the Conservatives) in convincing the electorate to give it another chance at governing. To what extend this is a result of the electorate finding itself increasingly at home with Centre-Right policies is something which will be explored further in the next section.

CLASS DEALIGNMENT

In Chapter 3, we examined the relationship between a person's vote and the social class from which they derive. In the 1950s and 1960s, there was a general agreement that this was the single most significant factor of all. Other factors such as gender, age, religion and geographical location failed to come near to the importance of social class.

There was no evidence of perfect class voting (in other words, of all the working class voting Labour and of all the middle class voting Conservative), but instead there were so-called 'deviant voters'. Indeed, given the relative size of the working and middle classes, the Conservative Party can be thankful for these deviants, otherwise it is likely that it would have been continuously out of office in the postwar period.

To what extent is there evidence of a breakdown in the relationship between social class and vote after 1970? In 1964, Labour had the support of 64 per cent of the working-class vote. By 1983, this had fallen to 42 per cent. The Conservatives did not fare as badly: in the same period, their share of the middle-class vote fell by only 7 per cent (from 62 to 55). So it would appear that there was change, and this seemed to affect the Labour Party more than it did the Conservatives.

There are other ways of measuring the change in class voting. Perhaps the best known is the **Alford Index**, which is calculated by simple subtraction. For Labour, simply subtract Labour's percentage share of the middle class (non-manual workers) from its share of the working class (manual workers). So, if Labour has 66 per cent of the working-class support and only 25 per cent of the middle-class support, then its index is 41. The higher the figure (up to maximum of 100), the greater the degree of class voting. The Conservative figures are calculated the opposite way round (by deducting the percentage of working-class share of their vote from the middle-class share of the vote).

Between 1964 and 1983, Labour's score for the Alford Index fell from 42 to 25 (a fall of 40 per cent), while the Conservative score fell from 34 to 20 (a 41-per-cent fall) over the same period. The figures flatten out in the later 1980s and early 1990s. Clearly, therefore, there has been a decline in class voting during the 1960s and 1970s. By the early 1980s, social class was no longer the predictor that it had once been. Indeed, in 1983, social class was less likely to be able to predict a person's vote than the toss of a coin.

What were the reasons for the desertion of so many voters from their natural party of class? Were these desertions temporary or a more permanent feature? Where were the new homes of these votes, and could they be relied upon to stay put?

REASONS FOR CLASS DEALIGNMENT

Increasing affluence
Some of the reasons used to explain the weakening of partisanship can help explain the reasons for class dealignment, and vice versa. The debate over the weakening of the influence of social class is not a new one, however. In the 1960s, Goldthorpe *et al.* attempted to measure the impact of working-class **affluence**, among Luton car workers, upon Labour Party support. (The resulting book was entitled *The Affluent Worker*.) They found no evidence at the time that this affluence was likely to lead to the abandonment of the Labour Party.

By the 1980s, however, there would appear to be some greater claim that affluence was an important factor. By this time, many more working-class people owned their own homes, owned a car (maybe two), owned shares and took foreign holidays. While it is not suggested that all this will turn a person into a card-carrying Conservative, it is perhaps going to make the 'property-owning, share-owning democracy' message of the Conservatives in the 1980s more resonant to a greater number of people, working-class ones included.

The changing middle-class structure
The above point may offer some indication as to why some working-class people have been willing to desert the Labour Party. What about the middle class and the Conservatives? It seems doubtful that in a period of increasing affluence, where working-class voters are discovering the merits of a market economy, members of the middle class are deserting this cause for Labour and the Liberals. The structure of the middle class has changed, however. It is no longer the

THE INCREASING AFFLUENCE OF THE WORKING CLASS IN THE 1980s, AS PORTRAYED BY DEREK TROTTER (DAVID JASON) IN THE BBC SIT-COM 'ONLY FOOLS AND HORSES'.

preserve of bankers, solicitors, clerks and doctors. In the 1960s and 1970s, there was a huge growth in public-sector professionals (teachers, social workers, educational psychologists, lecturers etc.) A large proportion of this group of workers will have had a natural 'communion of interest' with the Left in British politics, and the Labour Party is probably where many would offer their support.

Changing occupational structures

These changes have not been restricted to the middle class, however. There have been much wider changes in the occupational structures of Britain. These may have had a profound influence on British politics. Denver (1994) argues three trends worthy of note:

1 a shift from manual to non-manual work
2 a shift from manufacturing to the service sector
3 within manufacturing, a particularly severe decline in traditional, heavy industries, such as steel, coal and shipbuilding.

Patrick Dunleavy has suggested that the old occupational cleavage of manual/non-manual workers is becoming less important. The old class system is being replaced by a new one based upon one's position in the public and private sector.

According to this theory, an individual, working in the public sector, whose children go to state schools and whose family is reliant upon state benefits is more likely to support the Labour Party than a person working and consuming predominantly in the private sector (ie working in the private sector, owning their own home, sending their children to private schools and having private healthcare) (Dunleavy, 1980).

This picture is further complicated by those who do not conform to a stereotypical working- or middle-class set of characteristics. It may be that a person has a manual job but owns their own home. It may be that a couple lives in council accommodation, with the husband working in a manual occupation, and the wife in a non-manual job. It may be argued that, as increasing numbers of people are affected by the forces of more than one social class, the influence of either one of them is likely to be diluted – known as cross-class location (see page 18).

Even within a single social class, there may be differences which are likely to have an impact upon political behaviour. Crewe, writing in the early 1980s, argues that within the working class, two distinct camps can be discerned: a traditional working class, characterised by those in public-sector manual jobs, living in a council house in the North; and a new working class of manual workers in the private sector in their own homes in the South. It has been argued that in the former group, support for the Labour Party remained strong but that in the latter group, this support was much weaker.

Many of the points made above are now somewhat academic. In the 1980s and 1990s, they were often used as part of Labour Party obituaries, in explanation of how and why it would meet its eventual end. Unfortunately for some, these obituaries were somewhat premature. Indeed, the revival of Labour's fortunes has been accomplished by tapping into the reserves of working-class voters who own their own homes, have shares in British Telecom and work in the private sector.

Furthermore, part of the Labour Party's success in 1997 had to do not only with being able to recapture the votes of those who had deserted them for Margaret Thatcher in 1979 but also with attracting those who had never voted Labour before in their lives. In this respect, the metaphorical boot was on the other foot: it was the Conservatives who suffered the mass desertion.

The old certainties about class and vote have become very unreliable predictors of voting intentions. The quote from Peter Pulzer, in Chapter 3, when he said that anything other than class was '... embellishment and detail', comes to mind. In the 30 years since he wrote those words, the relationships between individuals and social class have become too complex to generalise and difficult to explain in terms of voting behaviour.

At this point, a number of issues need to be discussed to put some of the above points in context.

VOLATILITY

The word volatility has been used on numerous occasions in this and the previous chapter. I have been careful not to overuse the term 'voter volatility' as there is some debate in academic circles as to the extent of this. Pippa Norris (1997) suggests that there was indeed voter volatility in Britain in the early 1970s, but that after this time there were no trends which could be discerned. Rather, there were 'trendless fluctuations' which could be observed in the late 1970s and throughout the 1980s. To some extent, the 1997 General Election offered the best evidence for a volatile electorate since the early 1970s, the swing from the Conservatives to Labour being the biggest by far since 1945 (Denver, 1997).

Perhaps the term 'political volatality' should be used to indicate a phenomenon which is wider than voting behaviour. Simply limiting one's analysis of volatility to the size of electoral swings when a relatively small swing can have had such a major impact on the distribution of seats in the House of Commons in the 1980s and 1990s, is too narrowly focused an approach. Furthermore, the present era has been characterised by major social, economic and political change. The effects of our membership of the European Union, the major economic upheavals of the 1970s and 1980s and the changes in the political parties are all bound to have made a significant impact on the behaviour of voters and politicians alike.

SOCIAL CLASS — A REDEFINITION

In the mid-1980s, a major challenge was made to the dealignment thesis, the most prominent advocate of which was Ivor Crewe. In their book *How Britain Votes*, Heath, Jowell and Curtice sought to offer an alternative analysis to the question of class dealignment. Heath *et al.* offered a redefined classification of occupations, claiming that the one being used by many other writers was effectively out of date. Their new classification, the **'salariat'**, put salaried professionals into one group, self-employed persons into another, a third group was described as routine non-manual, the fourth as blue-collar supervisors and technicians, and the final group as rank and file working-class people. After using their schema, Heath *et al.* concluded that the relationship between class and vote has not been eroded in any systematic manner, and that no dealignment trend may be discerned.

There is insufficient space in this book to offer a meaningful analysis of their work. There have been a number of very forthright attacks on it, most notably from those expounding the theories that are being criticised in *How Britain Votes*. Ivor Crewe's (1986) is a notable example of such criticism.

SUMMARY

Overall, the level of partisanship has hardly changed over the past 35 years. Individuals are still prepared to link themselves with a particular political party.

There has, however, been a decline in the strength of partisanship. Voters have a significantly less strong attachment to their party than was the case a generation ago.

Overall, voters appear better informed about politics. The impact of television in particular has exposed voters to the bad side of their favoured party and possibly also to the good side of the party which they would not normally support.

It may be argued that an increasingly educated electorate has also helped to break down the old alignments.

After 40 years of promises, perhaps the electorate has wised up to our politicians and now treats their public utterances with the suspicion that they probably deserve. Voters, however, are not blameless here: by making ever-high demands on governments, they have perhaps harboured unrealistic expectations as to what can actually be achieved in an economy which for much of the postwar era has been in relative economic decline.

Of particular concern to Labour was evidence suggesting that traditional leftwing policies, such as nationalisation, were losing their popularity among Labour's traditional supporters.

Evidence also exists that some breakdown in the relationship between class and vote was taking place. By the 1980s, a smaller percentage of the working class was supporting the Labour Party and a smaller percentage of the middle class was supporting the Conservatives.

In the 1979 General Election, there was evidence for a switch in support from Labour to the Conservatives among members of the skilled working class (the so-called C2s).

A working class which has become more affluent is one explanation for this trend. As people purchase their own homes, buy shares and take foreign holidays, it may be argued that they are likely to find a greater resonance with the messages of the Conservative Party.

The middle class has expanded in the last two decades to include large numbers of public-sector professionals (teachers, social workers, lecturers and the like). It may be argued that the effect of these workers will be to 'water down' the traditional rock-solid support that it once had for the Conservatives.

Labour would appear to have benefited not only from a return of those voters who had deserted them in the late 1970s but also from the attraction of traditional, middle-class Conservative voters, many of whom may have never voted for the Labour Party in their lives.

STUDY GUIDES

Revision Hints

The dealignment thesis is crucial, not just to revising voting behaviour but also when looking at topics such as the impact of the mass media and changes to the organisation and policies of the political parties.

It may be tempting to concentrate on changes to the structure, composition and behaviour of the working class. Remember that there have been important developments in the middle class, which have affected both the Conservative and Labour Parties.

It is essential that you use up-to-date information. Analysis of the results of the 1997 General Election should be used.

Remember that there is the alternative thesis of Heath, Jowell and Curtice which challenges some the key assumptions of the proponents of dealignment.

Exam Hints

- You are unlikely to get straightforward questions such as 'What is partisan alignment?' Rather, you will be expected to weave this concept into an answer in a relevant and appropriate manner.
- In examining the influence of the media, partisan dealignment is an important factor in a number of respects. It has been weakened by the influence of television; and this in turn has helped to make readers more receptive to the views of the newspapers they read.
- Remember to offer the alternative analysis of dissenting voices. As mentioned above, some research has been conducted which does not concur with the conclusions about dealignment. These views may or may not have been effectively refuted in your own mind; whichever is the case, they should nonetheless be cited to let the examiner know that you are aware of differing interpretations of a particular topic.

Practice Questions

1 Why did partisan alignment become important after 1970?
2 Why were the C2s so important in the 1979 General Election?
3 Why did some commentators believe that Labour was a doomed political force after 1992?
4 Outline:
  a two factors which caused partisan dealignment;
  b two factors which caused class dealignment.

6

THE IMPACT OF
THE MEDIA

Introduction

THIS CHAPTER WILL look at the impact of the newspapers and television on voting behaviour. It will consider first the era of alignment, 1950–1970, during which it is claimed that the press tended to reinforce existing political attitudes; and then the era of dealignment, from 1970 onwards, where the issue of whether the press follows or forms public opinion is considered. Finally, there is a brief discussion about the media revolution to come over the next few years.

Key points
- The press and television in the era of alignment, 1950–1970.
- The press and television in the era of dealignment: 1970 onwards.
- The media revolution.

The media is a collective term which covers a whole range of communication means. This chapter will concentrate on newspapers and the broadcast media, particularly television.

The role of the media cannot be examined in isolation: there is a need to analyse it in the context of other issues raised in this book. The alignment/dealignment thesis, for example, is bound up inextricably with the issue of the media (see Chapter 5). It should become apparent, therefore, that the impact of the media has altered over time, and that much of the writing surrounding the media, particularly its impact at election times, has altered accordingly.

THE MEDIA IN THE ERA OF ALIGNMENT, 1950–1970

The forces at work at this time were clearly based upon the phenomena of class and partisan alignment. The question at stake, therefore, is to what extent there was room for newspapers and television to influence voting behaviour at a time when electoral choice was overwhelmingly determined by those social forces.

THE PRESS

Newspaper readership at this time displayed a marked correlation between the partisanship of the voter and that of the newspaper. For example, there has long been a strong level of support for the Labour Party by *The Mirror*. This correlation of support, however, is rather meaningless unless some explanation or line of causality can be established. Are *Mirror* readers influenced into voting for the Labour Party as a consequence of reading pro-Labour sentiments between the covers of that newspaper? Or alternatively, do individuals choose newspapers which are likely to agree with their own political inclinations, in which case the correlation of views almost becomes a self-fulfilling prophecy?

Butler and Stokes considered the role of the press carefully in their seminal study, and the nature of the relationship between the partisanship of newspapers and that of their readers led them to conclude that there was indeed a difficulty in establishing a line of causality (Butler and Stokes, 1974). They made the following observation:

> *The coincidence between a paper's partisanship and that of its readers is not of course, simply ascribable to the paper's stimulus and the reader's response; it may equally be due to the opposite process ... The distinctive partisan colouring of those who read the morning dailies could be taken as evidence of the press's influence only if it is clear that the choice of a newspaper preceded the choice of a party. But it is ... quite possible either for a paper to be chosen for its partisanship or for the choice of both paper and party to reflect the influence of a family or class milieu. In such a case, the press might play a role in conserving a party tie; it would not have created it.*

Butler and Stokes, 1974, p 117.

The evidence, at the height of the era of alignment, suggests that newspapers merely had the effect of **reinforcement** of existing political opinions. In other words, the sheer strength of the prevailing forces at this time left little room for newspapers to have any significant impact upon electoral behaviour. Where there *was* an impact, this *was* confined to those individuals who formed the relatively small army of **floating voters**.

Given that the large majority of voters at the time were aligned to one of the main political parties, this impact was relatively minor, and consequently it is difficult to ascribe much political influence to the press in this respect. Of course, this is not to suggest that newspapers exerted no influence at all in politics at the time. Newspaper editors were clearly in the business of influencing both politicians and, where it was possible, members of the voting public. It may be argued that floating voters, by definition, determine the outcome of elections, and so that even at this time, where the vast bulk of electors seemed inured to the impact of the press, a crucial few were open to its influence.

This impact must be put into broad perspective, however, given the large numbers of voters seemingly unaffected by the press. Butler and Stokes, having identified the strength of social and family ties, go on to conclude as follows:

> *If the voter's report on his family is accepted, it is clear that newspapers often profit from, rather than shape, their readers' party ties.*
>
> Butler and Stokes, 1974, p 118.

Denver identifies a '**Filter model**' of media influence which suggests the existence of a perceptual screen between the source of a message and the recipient (Denver, 1994). This screen enables individuals to be selective in what they see, hear or read. In this regard, voters are more likely to read a newspaper which already concurs with their own inclinations. Denver goes on to argue that the *selective exposure* is not the only consequence of the perceptual screen: selective perception also enables the individuals to screen out messages that they don't want to hear. Even reading a newspaper hostile to one's own party, therefore, is likely to have little impact. This is followed up by **selective retention** whereby individuals remember those messages which fit their own point of view (Denver, 1994).

TELEVISION

The era of alignment (1950–1970) witnessed the emergence of television from being the minority pastime of an elite few to a mass form of entertainment touching virtually everyone in society. The impact of television has been blamed on a whole range of social problems, and it has also been suggested that television bias has impacted upon voters. The evidence of these claims is often anecdotal, with little substantive evidence to back it up.

The difficulty with television lies with the statutory regulation within which the television organisations exist. The BBC is effectively governed by its Royal Charter which forbids any overt party political support. The independent television companies are regulated by an Act of Parliament which similarly restricts the nature of political coverage (in the case of the latter, for example, political advertising, such as is prevalent in the USA, is forbidden).

Before 1955, there was only one television channel available to viewers, and politics was a subject dealt with in a very respectful manner designed to offend no-one and therefore as a consequence unlikely to inform people much either. The arrival of ITV in 1955 did not result in an immediate revolution in the coverage of politics on television. Indeed, it was not until the General Election of 1959, by which time about three-quarters of the population owned a television set, that we saw the sort of coverage that is common at election time today.

It has been suggested that the abandonment of the deferential approach and the rise of such figures as Robin Day, willing to challenge politicians and their claims, did begin to weaken the partisanship of voters (see Chapter 5). There is no inference, however, that television has, either consciously or unconsciously, systematically shifted votes in a particular direction.

Research conducted during this period demonstrated both on the one hand the power that television has in overcoming the so-called 'filter effect', and on the other hand, however, its lack of influence in party political terms.

> *There was a significant increase in political knowledge during the campaign ... attempts to convey information do not [seem to] meet with the same resistance as does the attempt to persuade ...*
>
> *Political change was neither related to the degree of exposure nor to any particular programmes or arguments put forward by the parties ... The inter-election years become more important than the nineteen days of campaigning, however intensive, because the swing is almost entirely accounted for before the opening of the election campaign*
>
> Trenamen and McQuail, 1961, pp 232 & 128.

It may be argued that television at this time, like newspapers, had the effect of reinforcing existing political attitudes rather than changing them. It would seem to fit in with the model of aligned voting that factors other than social class and partisanship are unlikely to affect the large majority of the electorate in any significant way. The above quote, however, is quite time-specific: the study covered the 1959 General Election. This was a time when the aligned voting was at its strongest and television coverage of politics was in its infancy.

THE MEDIA IN AN ERA OF DEALIGNMENT

The long-term effect of television may be quite different. It has been argued in the previous chapter that increased political awareness, partly a result of television, was a contributing factor to the weakening of partisanship from the mid-1960s onwards. This has led to the electorate becoming more susceptible to political messages coming directly from the politicians' mouths and indirectly from political commentators on television.

THE PRESS

Of course, voters will become susceptible not only to television but also to other elements of the mass media. This is where we may return to the impact of the press. It has already been observed that during the period of class and partisan alignment, the press was probably unable to overcome the entrenched political beliefs of many in the electorate. Since the breakdown of these alignments, there is obviously more scope for newspapers to affect political views.

In the 1970s and 1980s, therefore, newspaper proprietors managed to achieve what they perhaps have always believed to be their ultimate destiny: to use their positions of power to influence the readers of their publications. For decades, it could be argued, the likes of Beaverbrook were merely thundering in resonance with their readership. After so long, readers, were beginning to listen to what the 'fourth estate' had to say.

These are all very generalised conclusions, however. Is there any concrete evidence to suggest that the press is now influencing public opinion? Perhaps more importantly as far as this book is concerned, does this evidence extend to voting in general elections?

Up until the General Election of 1992, the common appraisal of the situation was that newspapers had a reinforcing effect upon reader's political preferences. Some research had been undertaken to suggest that perhaps in the long term, there was some impact occurring (Curtice and Smetko, 1994). There was little to suggest that there were influences in the short term, say over the course of a three-week election campaign, or at least in the weeks running up to it. Indeed, the classical orthodoxy remained fairly consistent with the conclusions drawn by Trenamen and McQuail (see page 51), that elections are decided well before the opening of the campaign.

It has been suggested that the media may have an agenda-setting role. Perhaps newspapers and television do indeed determine what issues voters think about. There is some evidence from the USA that this may be the case, but in Britain, Miller has found little to support this. In the latter's study, there appeared to be little connection between the issues highlighted by the media and those considered important by voters (Miller, 1991).

Public opinion – following it or forming it?

The 1992 General Election led to a rethink of this appraisal. In the immediate aftermath of the result, it was understandable to dismiss the hyperbole of *The Sun's* headline 'It Wos the Sun Wot Won it', for here was a newspaper which had stuck by John Major and waged a savage attack on the Labour Party generally and its leader Neil Kinnock in particular. Alistair McAlpine, the then Conservative Party Treasurer, was effusive in his praise when he described the editors of the *Daily Express* and the *Daily Mail* as '... the heroes of the campaign'.

All this of course could be the understandable reaction of a party and its supporters who were trying to explain the unexpected victory.

Since then, firmer evidence has surfaced which indicates that these words contained more than a grain of truth. Martin Linton formerly of *The Guardian* has published the results of research which shows that there were indeed short-term shifts of votes in the months and weeks before election day in April 1992, and that these shifts were particularly evident among readers of Conservative-supporting newspapers. Linton's research showed that although the majority of *The Sun*'s readers were Labour supporters, they swung heavily to the Conservatives in the run-up to the election. In the three months before election day, data from ICM-MORI showed a swing of 8 per cent to the Conservatives among *Sun* readers, and of 0 per cent among readers of *The Mirror* (whose readers form a very similar social profile of those of *The Sun*).

The research also showed that there were swings to the Conservatives among readers of other Tory-supporting newspapers such as the *Daily Telegraph*, *Daily Express* and *Daily Mail*. The only daily newspapers to back Labour's 1992 bid for power were *The Mirror*, *The Guardian* and *The Financial Times*. Across the spectrum of daily newspapers, Linton calculates that the Conservatives had 70 per cent of the press behind them, with Labour at 27 per cent. Labour has never won an election when this **press deficit** has been greater than 18 per cent (in all the elections between 1945 and October 1974, this figure varied between 10 and 18 per cent. Between 1979 and 1992, it averaged 45 per cent) (Linton, 1995).

This situation may explain the strategy of New Labour since the election of Tony Blair as its leader. Blair's press secretary summed it up in an article for the magazine *Tribune*: 'Can we make the *Daily Mail* 10 per cent less hostile than it otherwise would be? Is there the tiniest possibility that the News International papers might back Labour?' (quoted in Linton, 1995).

Between 1994 and 1997, Blair wrote numerous articles for Murdoch's titles. He addressed a convention of News International executives on Murdoch's private island in Australia and did manage to woo some of Labour's oldest enemies in Fleet Street. On the day after the election was announced in March 1997, The Sun indeed did put its weight behind Blair, and some of the most hitherto rightwing titles, whilst not backing Labour, did not give the Conservatives the sort of adulatory support that they had enjoyed previously. It would appear at the very least that the sting had been taken out of the press's tail and that at best a few titles were lending their support.

PRESS FOLLOWING PUBLIC OPINION? *THE SUN* SWINGS TO SUPPORT FOR TONY BLAIR DURING THE 1997 GENERAL ELECTION CAMPAIGN.

It is tempting, after examining the impact of the press in the 1992 General Election, to extrapolate this to the 1997 result. It may be that Rupert Murdoch abandoned the Tories because he was convinced there was no hope for them. To back Labour was to back a winner (always a good thing to be seen doing), and there was of course the matter of cross-media ownership. Why risk supporting the Conservatives when, by supporting Labour, Murdoch was at least not going to antagonise a new Labour government who could do him quite considerable financial harm if it decided to limit media possessions? There is no evidence, however, to suggest that any deal was done on this matter.

The idea of the press *following* public opinion rather than *forming* it may seem quite novel to many observers, yet the industry itself attempts to dispel the conspiracy theories surrounding its power by claiming to respond to changes in the market. Certainly, Sir Larry Lamb, editor of *The Sun* at the time of the 1979 General Election, claims that his own paper's switch of allegiance to Margaret Thatcher was a consequence of the shifts of opinion being measured in surveys of its readership.

This may be uncharacteristic tabloid modesty or it may be the sober reflection that a newspaper, like any other business, wants both to keep its existing customers and to attract new ones. If this means adapting the product to reflect changing customer tastes, then that is the sign of a responsive entrepreneur. This point of view might be described as a smoke screen, an attempt to throw predators of the media off the scent. To simply put these shifts of opinion down to market forces is to be highly selective in ascribing good business practice to an industry which has often been guided by some very poor business practice in the past.

There is some disagreement about the line of causality between the shift in party support in 1979 and 1997 by newspapers such as *The Sun*. Did the newspapers influence the voters, or did the shift in voter opinion cause a switch in newspaper support? This debate might be an important one in another context, but it has already been revealed that in the 1992 General Election, a shift in opinion to the Conservative Party was measured among the existing readers of newspapers, and that this switch came *after* the editorials and comment columns offering support to the Conservatives. This puts the somewhat modest utterings of newspaper editors into context.

The television treatment

There is perhaps another way in which newspaper bias can exert influence on voters. This is through the somewhat surprising medium of television. Earlier in this chapter, it was mentioned that broadcasters are far more tightly regulated when it comes to the reporting of politics and these rules are even more rigid during the course of an election campaign. Yet, newspapers are only constrained by the laws of libel and slander (and even here, it may be argued that big chances are taken with the law). Newspapers and television sit side by side, reporting the same news, effectively feeding from the same pond. Stories which break on television usually get the 'tabloid treatment' the day after. Conversely, stories which originate in the columns of the press may often find themselves taken up and put on our TV screens.

The problem here is determining the motivation of a particular newspaper in publishing a story, and this is especially the case during an election campaign. When, in 1983, *The Sun* sent a series of quotes by the Labour MP Tony Benn to an American psychiatrist for analysis, the paper revelled in the wholly spurious conclusions which were arrived at in the blind analysis. Broadcasters, however, quite easily see this for what is: crude character assassination aimed at sullying a political party. Understandably, this story did not migrate from the pages of *The Sun* onto *News at Ten*. During the 1970s, however, a series of serious accusations involving government ministers and appointees, originating in the press, rocked the Labour government. Cabinet minister Ted Short was accused of having money, obtained by dubious means, lying in secret Swiss bank accounts. Of course, the story spilled onto the television, and Short's position became untenable. Ted Short fought and in the end succeeded in clearing his name, but it was too late: his government career was over.

This may be a somewhat melodramatic example to use, and thankfully there are not too many of these to relate. In an age, however, where the press can pass comment off as fact, it is all too easy for news-hungry broadcasters to relate stories which are dubious of origin at best and outright pernicious party propaganda at worst. Without care, broadcastors could become the unwitting accomplices of newspapers whose agendas are far more overtly party political.

THE MEDIA REVOLUTION

The measurement of media impact on politics is often difficult and fraught with risks. The aim of this chapter has not been to offer scientific proof of the impact of the media, for none exists. Instead, there has been an attempt to identify the differences between different strands of the media and to offer an analysis based on political change. The truths and certainties of a generation ago no longer pertain today. In recent years, we have seen the explosion of information on the Internet, and no doubt studies will appear in due course offering analysis of the Web and its impact on politics in Britain. Certainly, the political parties have not been slow to make their presence felt on the Internet, all three major ones having very sophisticated sites.

In the next few years, a media revolution will take place in Britain. With the onset of digital broadcasting in the Autumn of 1998, television viewers will eventually be able to tune in to hundreds of channels, many devoted to current affairs. As these channels proliferate, the job of regulating output will become ever more difficult. The challenge for the broadcasters will be to maintain the political neutrality of their news and current affairs, and it may be a challenge in which they cannot succeed. If this is the case, then the entire set of assumptions that is made about the impact of the media will become redundant. The textbooks and chapters about the media's powers to influence political attitudes and voting behaviour will have to be rewritten.

SUMMARY

With aligned voting, the scope for media impact on electoral behaviour is limited.

The press may be seen in terms of reinforcing existing political attitudes. Readers of *The Mirror* may be overwhelmingly sympathetic to the Labour Party, and this is likely to have affected their choice of paper, rather than vice versa.

At this time, there may of course have been as effect on floating voters. This group, however, formed a relatively small percentage of the electorate during the 1950s and 1960s.

It has been argued that, when confronted with newspapers hostile to their own political beliefs, voters 'filter out' messages they don't want to see or hear.

Television is a newer medium. News and current-affairs coverage here only started to take on a recognisable form in the late 1950s and early 1960s. Broadcast journalism is much more tightly regulated than the press.

Research in the early 1960s showed that television, whilst an important source of political information, had little or no direct effect on political attitudes.

The long term effect of television is not quite so neutral. It is argued that it helped weaken partisanship, thus increasing the receptivity of viewers to the impact of other mediums such as the press.

Research has shown that the press might have had a decisive impact on voters in the 1992 General Election campaign.

Labour's attempts to reach an accommodation with the press have been attributed to its desire to neutralise hostility and bias.

The press claims to *respond to* reader demand rather than attempting to *change* their opinions (the research on the 1992 election tends to limit this argument, however).

Stories originating in the press find their way onto television screens. Perhaps, politically motivated stories manage to receive a loud echo in this manner.

The future of television threatens to undermine the coverage of politics, which hitherto has been characterised by balance and neutrality.

Revision Hints

This topic is relevant to elements in the core module, to questions about factors influencing voting behaviour, and to optional module questions about the impact of the mass media. Clearly, this is a very important topic to revise.

A lot of media-based examination questions are poorly answered. Many candidates seem to believe that it is not important to revise this topic thoroughly, relying instead on a generalised understanding of the media. Sadly, these responses owe more to tabloid journalism and afternoon talk shows than to any fundamental grasp of the topic. This topic should be revised in as systematic and rigorous a manner as any other on the syllabus.

Ensure that you gather statistical evidence about the impact of the press and television.

Exam Hints

- Do not answer a question on the media if all you have are vague, generalised observations to offer. Such basic-level responses stand out, and they receive little reward. Answering a question in this manner could seriously harm your overall examination mark (and grade!).
- The use of quotations and statistical evidence in this area is essential. Given that many candidates will be relying upon half-remembered (and therefore probably inaccurate) headlines, the use of hard evidence can raise your answer above the norm for answers to questions on this topic.
- Many questions focus on the *changing* impact of the media. Examine the dynamics of the topic, by comparing and contrasting different periods.
- Questions often require separate treatment of different mediums. Ensure you know what is being asked of you. For example, if you are required to examine the influence of the press and television, devote space to each of these. Offer points specific to each medium to show the examiner that you are capable of evaluating between the two.

Practice Questions

1 Distinguish between the impact of television and newspapers on British public opinion.
2 Compare and contrast the influence of the press in the elections of 1992 and 1997.
3 To what extent are the media
  a biased
  b powerful?
4 'Newspapers reinforce the existing political views of their readers.' Discuss.

7

VOTING TRENDS AND ELECTORAL REFORM

Introduction

THIS CHAPTER WILL offer a summary of voting behaviour as given over the last five chapters – looking at the two-party period and the period of increasing political instability – and then discuss the issue of electoral reform as an introduction to subsequent chapters on electoral systems.

Key points
- Summary of voting trends.
- Electoral reform.

SUMMARY OF VOTING TRENDS

The previous five chapters have attempted to outline and explain the major changes in voting behaviour over the past half century. In a book of this size, full justice cannot be done to the amount of research that has been conducted by academics over these years. For this reason, these chapters offer only a flavour of the work that has been carried out. Readers will find details of further reading at the end of the book.

THE TWO-PARTY SYSTEM

It has been argued that, between 1950 and 1970, Britain had a stable two-party system. Both the Conservative and Labour parties were regularly capable of commanding a combined share of over 90 per cent of the votes in elections during this time. This dominance in votes was matched by a dominance in seats, and although there was disproportionality in evidence, third parties were so insignificant for much of this period that the question of electoral reform did not feature on the political agenda.

The main explanation for this stable two-party system was that of alignments in partisanship and social class. The majority of voters were quite strongly psychologically attached to what they considered to be the natural party of their social class, and this attachment was unlikely to be shaken by issues and events.

POLITICAL INSTABILITY – DEALIGNMENT

After 1970, the picture changes significantly and with surprising speed. In the election of 1974, Labour and the Conservatives saw their combined share of the vote fall by 15 per cent. Support for other parties grew, with the Liberals taking nearly one fifth of the vote and the Scottish National Party taking 30 per cent of the vote in Scotland. The once-solid two-party edifice seemed to have cracked. The quite exceptional events of the early 1970s: the world oil crisis, the domestic industrial unrest and the three-day week, may be offered as a partial explanation for the suddenness of the shift in opinion. What is truly exceptional, however, is the way that support was lost by both the government and the main party of opposition. It was as if the voters had lost confidence in the political system.

There were forces at work, however, that go further back than 1970, so although the events of 1970–1974 were contributory factors to the scale of the changes, the context of what was happening to the certainties of the old alignments must be emphasised.

The two great anchors which had steadied the political system in Britain appeared to be giving way. Voters were weakening in their partisanship, and the link between social class and voting behaviour was declining in significance. It has been shown that factors such as the influence of television were important in explaining the weakening of party identification; and the impact of social class was declining as the occupational structure of the country changed: more and more families failed to conform to the traditional stereotypes of either the middle class or the working class.

Nature abhors a vacuum, and with decline of social class and partisanship, there came the notable rise in influence of the media, and, as a consequence, of the major political issues that go reported. What is in evidence here is dealignment, the breakdown of traditional influences on voting behaviour. There is no evidence for a realignment in British politics, and it would seem – though the evidence for this is somewhat mixed – that we are left with a volatile and unstable political system. The implications for the political parties were profound: Labour was confined to opposition for the 1980s and most of the 1990s, and only after major organisational reforms and policy changes has it been able to return to power. The Conservatives, by the early 1990s, must have believed that the changes had permanently led to their winning power. The result of the 1997 General Election was a powerful message to the contrary. Perhaps the very forces that swept them to power in 1979 and kept them there for 18 years were the very same ones which were to shatter them so decisively on that fateful first day of May.

The impact of dealignment on the third parties was perhaps in the long run more portentous. The rise of the Scottish Nationalists and Plaid Cymru was to lead to two governments' introducing legislation for devolved government in Scotland and Wales. While the first ended with the fall of the Labour government of James Callaghan in 1979, it would appear that the second will at least have a chance to be tested in practice.

The Centre parties in British politics since 1970 have had more mixed fortunes. The Liberals and the SDP were able to command up to a quarter of the national vote but have never made significant inroads in winning seats in the House of Commons. Ironically, the Liberal Democrats more than doubled their number of MPs in May 1997 on a *reduced* share of the vote compared to 1992. The result has been to raise the profile of the debate about electoral reform on the political agenda.

ELECTORAL REFORM

Clearly, the Liberals, then the Alliance and now the Liberal Democrats, have maintained their opposition to a system which appears to be an increasingly randomised way of electing a chamber of representatives. Other organisations such as the Electoral Reform Society and Charter 88 have added their voices to the calls for reform.

These calls went largely unheard during the 1970s, 1980s and most of the 1990s, mainly because the governing party of the day saw nothing but political disadvantage resulting from electoral reform. Even in opposition in the 1980s, Labour maintained a common stance with the Conservatives, opposed to any change. A growing number of Labour MPs were supporters of reform, however, and the debate going on in the party led to the establishing of the Plant Commission, which reported in 1991. Within the party, the calls for change have grown louder. In office, Labour has legislated for proportional elements to the voting systems to be used in elections to the Scottish Parliament and Welsh Assembly, as well as in elections to the European Parliament from 1999 onwards. Most significantly, the government is also considering changes to the way Westminster elections take place, and the person who chaired the deliberation, Lord Jenkins of Hillhead, is himself a convinced adherent of proportional representation.

The Conservatives continue to oppose the principle of electoral reform – even though the party would have had around 50 extra MPs if a proportional system had been in use when it lost power. However, there are a small number of MPs in the Conservative Party who are in favour of some reform of the voting system. Perhaps if the party suffers a second election defeat, there will be an increase in the number of Conservatives who favour a reformed system.

The debate about electoral reform is well worn. Perhaps as significant, however, is the debate within the pro-reform lobby about which system should be introduced. The remainder of this book will be spent examining the options which are available and what constitute their main strengths and weaknesses. To help explain the workings of the system, a case study is provided for each of them, and there will be an attempt to conclude on their suitability for Britain.

8

THE FIRST-PAST-THE-POST SYSTEM

Introduction

THIS CHAPTER WILL look at the first-past-the-post electoral system. It will consider how it works, its impact and the British party system, and the main arguments in favour of the system: strong and stable government; single-party government; the simplicity of the system; and constituency representation.

Key points

- How the first-past-the-post system works.
- Its impact on the British party system.
- Main arguments in its favour.

This system may also be known as the **plurality system** or the **simple majority system**. It is used in elections, most notably in Canada, India, Britain and the USA. Up until recently, it was also the electoral system of New Zealand.

HOW IT WORKS

This system is clearly the one most familiar to British and US readers. The plurality formula states that, in the case of **single-member constituencies**, voters may cast only one vote, and the candidate who obtains the most votes wins. In the case of two-member constituencies, voters have two votes, and in such cases, the two candidates who come in first and second place, each win. The following uses the British example to illustrate how the system operates in practice.

This system is very easy to understand, being without the need to express a relative preference for the candidates on offer, and being unreliant upon relatively complicated quotas for the count. In Britain, the elections to the House of Commons take place in 659 constituencies, each electing a single member. The same system is used in local government elections and elections to the European Parliament (with a different system operating in Northern Ireland). By-elections can be held in an individual constituency in the period between general elections if, for example, an MP dies or wishes to resign.

This is essentially the same process as existed over a century ago when voters elected their representatives by a show of hands. Since then, there has been the introduction of the **secret ballot** and legislation to control corrupt practices, as well as measures to extend the franchise to the working class, women and the 18–20 age group. By contrast, there has been no significant reform of the electoral system during this time.

WHO WINS?

The result of an election using the FPTP system needs to be measured in two ways: in the first place, at the constituency level, and second when adding up all the constituency results to get an overall state of the parties in the House of Commons.

In the constituency, the result is arrived at by simply counting all the votes for each candidate. Indeed, as far as the overall result is concerned, the only place where the number of votes count is at the constituency level. As far as the national result is concerned, there is merely an aggregation of seats won by the various political parties. Figure 13 shows one of the results (for Crawley) for the 1997 General Election. This result shows that in the First Past the Post system, Laura Moffatt, the Labour Party candidate, won the seat, taking over half of all the votes cast.

CRAWLEY
Lab Gain from C
Electorate 69,040. Turnout 50,417 (73.03%)

Laura Moffatt (Lab)..........27,750   **(55.04%)**
Josephine Crabb (C) 16,043   (31.82%)
Harold de Souza (LD)............4,141   (8.21%)
Ronald Walters (Ref) 1,931   (3.83%)
Eric Saunders (UK Ind)............322   (0.64%)
Arshad Kahn (JP)......................230   (0.46%)
Lab Maj 11,707
1992 C maj 1,890

FIGURE 13: THE 1997 GENERAL ELECTION RESULT FOR THE CRAWLEY CONSTITUENCY

A characteristic of this system is that all votes for the other candidates are effectively wasted. In the case of the Crawley constituents, there is at least the point that the elected representative obtained over half the vote. In many constituencies, however, this is not the case, as Figure 14, for Bristol West, illustrates. In the case of the Bristol West, the winning candidate was well short of half of the vote. Indeed, those opposing the Labour candidate amounted to nearly two-thirds of the vote. In the 1997 election, there were a number of constituencies where the winning candidate obtained less than half of the total vote. The implications of this from a mathematical point of view are quite alarming since it means that a government is being returned with a majority of seats in the House of Commons, but that these seats do not represent a majority of the national vote. Indeed, Tony Blair's landslide victory, like many before,was achieved with substantially less than half the total vote (44.5 per cent in fact).

BRISTOL WEST
Lab Gain from C
Electorate 84,870. Turnout 62,641 (73.81%)

Valerie Davey (Lab) ....22,068 **(35.23%)**
William Waldegrave (C) 20,575 (32.85%)
Charles Boney (LD) 17,551 (28.02%)
Margot Beauchamp (Ref)......1,304 (2.08%)
Justin Quinnell (Green) 852 (1.36%)
Roy Nurse (Soc Lab)................244 (0.39%)
Jai Brierley (NLP) 47 (0.08%)
Lab Maj 1,493
1992 C maj 9,494

FIGURE 14: THE 1997 GENERAL ELECTION RESULT FOR THE BRISTOL WEST CONSTITUENCY

The manner in which the FPTP system enables the formation of a government has therefore led to further controversy. In the 1950s and 1960s, governments were being elected with less than half the vote but within 1 to 3 per cent of that figure. By the 1970s, the figure was between 6 and 13 per cent below, again placing the system in the line of some very critical fire.

THE IMPACT ON THE BRITISH PARTY SYSTEM

This section in subsequent chapters will be mainly a crystal-ball-gazing exercise. On this occasion, it is much easier to comment upon the impact of the FPTP system on the political landscape in Britain.

Since 1945, the British political system has been dominated by two political parties. Both Labour and especially the Conservatives have enjoyed periods in government during this time. Many politicians regard this is as partly a consequence of the voting system, although as earlier chapters have pointed out, social factors did for a long time determine the way people voted in elections. It could be argued that the nature of the electoral system and the nature of class voting were in some respects entwined, but this is really beyond the remit of this book.

THE SINGLE-MEMBER CONSTITUENCY

Is it possible to isolate the consequences of our electoral system? There are a number of areas which can be identified. First, there is no question that the nature of the **single-member constituency** has created a mindset among politicians, academics and some members of the public of the importance of the constituency-based MP. So much is this the case that it is doubtful that any reform of the electoral system is likely to do away with this feature, and this, therefore, automatically begins to eliminate the options available.

MAJORITY GOVERNMENT

Another consequence has been that of majority government. In all but one election between 1945 and 1997, there has been a government elected with a Parliamentary majority (although it must be admitted straight away that there have been a few others that have come rather close to not being so elected). It is doubtful, voting habits remaining equal, that there would have been majority governments had another system of election been in place.

A corollary of the two-party dominance of the postwar years has been the difficulties encountered by smaller political parties. The Liberals, Liberal–SDP Alliance and latterly the Liberal Democrats have failed to make the inroads that their level of support suggests they could. Against this, one should be reminded of the position of the Scottish National Party and the manner in which this small party used the electoral system to its advantage by concentrating on campaigning in a coherent and limited number of seats. Related to this point is the 1997 election performance of the Liberal Democrats, who by concentrating its electoral machine on a number of target seats, were able to more than double their representation in the House of Commons (paradoxically on a reduced vote compared to their 1992 performance).

Indeed, the argument over the negative impact of the FPTP system on small parties is even more suspect when one looks at the performance of these parties in local government elections. In this arena, third parties, and in particular the Liberal Democrats, have a much higher profile. Yet local government uses precisely the same electoral system as is used in national elections. Clearly, there is a difference of perception among voters between electing councillors on the one hand and electing MPs on the other. This altered perception is what should perhaps be the subject of greater research rather than the automatic and, on occasions perhaps, spurious assumed exact correlation between the working of the electoral system and the performance of smaller parties. At the very least, this correlation is not a perfect one.

THE MAIN ARGUMENTS FOR AND AGAINST THE SYSTEM

There has been a tendency for the main supporters and opposers of this system to cleave along lines of those likely to fare best and least well out of the system. It is no surprise therefore that the Liberals and latterly the Liberal Democrats have been some of the severest critics of the system. Conversely, the Conservatives have rejected change out of hand (although there is a pro-reform movement within the party).

Labour has undergone something of a change on the issue in recent years. Although there has always been a reformist contingent among Labour MPs and supporters, during the years of the Conservative governments from 1979 to 1997, greater support for reform of the electoral system has become evident. In the late 1980s and early 1990s, the then Labour leader Neil Kinnock set up a committee under the chairmanship of Professor Raymond (now Lord) Plant to investigate reform. Some cynical opinion might attribute this more to the fact that by the early 1990s and three successive general-election defeats, Labour found it hard to see how it could win again under the existing system. A more measured response would be that by this time the reformist elements of the party, including former Labour-opposition front bencher Bryan Gould and the present Labour Foreign Secretary Robin Cook, had aspired to prominence within the Parliamentary Labour Party. Tony Blair, however, 'remains unconvinced' of the case for electoral reform.

Since the election of the Labour government in 1997, there has been a major flurry of activity on the issue of electoral reform. The successful referendums for devolved assemblies in Scotland and Wales have been followed by legislation which provides for proportional representation for elections to these assemblies. The elections to the European Parliament in 1999 were fought in the UK using a system of proportional representation. After the success of the 'Yes' campaign in the referendum on the Good Friday peace initiative, elections to the new Northern Ireland Assembly were also contested on proportional lines.

Many critics or cynics argue that this approach typifies all British governments, who offer electoral reform where it does not matter, where no real power will be exercised (after all, Tony Blair did admit during the 1997 General Election campaign that devolved assemblies in Scotland and Wales could be seen as little more than '... glorified parish councils'). To counter this point, however, it should be noted that Tony Blair himself asked the Liberal Democrat peer, Lord Jenkins of Hillhead (the former Labour cabinet minister Roy Jenkins), to head a commission to investigate and recommend an electoral system for elections to the House of Commons. The idea is then to hold a referendum on the proposal.

The debate on electoral reform will continue to be a heated one. Whichever sides are adopted by the political parties, the arguments in defence of and in opposition to the FPTP system are usually the same. Those defending the system usually highlight four main points, namely that the present system had led to:

- strong and stable government
- single-party government
- a system the people can understand
- **constituency representation**

STRENGTH AND STABILITY

Britain is usually singled out in this debate as one of the few countries with a strong and stable political system, which derives in part from our electoral system. The fact that there have been so few coalition governments in our history (and none since 1945) shows us to be the envy of countries such as Italy which has had scores of governments since the end of the Second World War. This rapid turnover of administrations has meant that few have been successful in enacting their electoral programmes. In any case, defenders of the FPTP system emphasise that the nature of coalition government effectively stifles strong government. In Britain, with governments lasting on average four years in between general elections, there is relative stability in the political system. As a result, governments are able, with few exceptions, to get their legislative programmes through Parliament, and it is rare for governments to lose legislation in adverse votes in the House of Commons. It is almost unheard of for governments to be defeated in votes of confidence in the House of Commons (the only occasion since 1945 was in March 1979, which caused the fall of the Callaghan Labour government).

Table 8 gives an indication of the strength of government majorities during the period.

Some unstable periods

The problem with the above analysis is that so many assumptions are made about politics in Britain and too restricted a view is taken of overseas examples as to make it somewhat suspect.

Stable government has been defined as governments with large majorities effectively preventing political uncertainty. Further analysis of the postwar period, however, shows a number of occasions where government majorities have been so small or non-existent as to make them vulnerable not only to the attacks of the opposition but also to internal sniping from within the governing party itself. The following periods have proved troubled ones for governments during these times:

- Feb 1950 to Oct 1951
- Oct 1964 to Mar 1966
- Feb 1974 to May 1979
- Apr 1992 to May 1997

Table 8: *Government majorities in British general elections*	
GENERAL ELECTION	GOVERNMENT MAJORITY (SEATS)
1945	144
1950	4
1951	16
1955	58
1959	100
1964	4
1966	96
1970	30
Feb 1979	–17
Oct 1974	3
1979	42
1983	144
1987	102
1992	21
1997	179

The implication of the list of unstable periods is that out of the 47 years covered by this book, over 13 (nearly one-third of the total time) were occupied by governments which did not appear particularly stable. (Some argument may occur about when precisely the Major government became thus.) The Heath government of 1972–74 was itself also a precarious administration, but this was the result of factors *outside* Parliament – namely industrial unrest and trade-union activity – rather than of any intrinsic instability in the government itself.

Thus, while not challenging the thesis that the period was mainly stable, the notion that it was overwhelmingly so should be.

Strong government not so virtuous?
Given that two-thirds of the past 47 years has seen stable governments, it may also be assumed that this proportion also saw years of strong government. This is not an unreasonable assumption. What may be challenged, however, is the virtue of such strength given some governments' innate capacity to harm, and the value of such strength when looked at in contrast to some overseas examples (which will be examined in later chapters). The above situation is further complicated by the existence of de-facto coalition governments during the course of the twentieth century (see page 71).

Strong government is applauded as a virtue in politics. It means governments being able to get a legislative programme through. It is interesting, however, to listen very carefully to the proponents of this view. Consider the large Parliamentary majority achieved by the Conservatives in 1983, which was staunchly defended by Conservative ministers and MPs alike as a means of carrying forward the Thatcherite agenda. In 1997, many of those same voices were attacking the size of the Labour government's majority for leading to the 'arrogance of power'. Similarly, read what prominent members of the Labour Party said in 1983 and 1997. What is clear is that strength only appears to be a virtue when one's own party is in office.

SINGLE-PARTY GOVERNMENT

It is common to characterise British government as being single-party in nature, and then perhaps tempting to ascribe such a characteristic to the FPTP system. Indeed, since 1900 there have been only 13½ years during which the country has been governed by coalition, and eight and a half of those years were wartime governments. In peacetime, then, only five years this century have seen what David Butler describes as ' ... clear and explicit coalition government' (Butler, 1978).

Other-party influences and internal factions

The nature of British party government is in some danger of being oversimplified, however. It may be true that for most of the time, the country has enjoyed single-party government, but the analysis in the previous section has shown that for a significant period, this has not equated with strong government. Indeed, the five years of coalition government indicated above are somewhat misleading. Butler has indicated a number of periods of government in this century where the government might have been overwhelmingly dominated by one party but where there was at least the influence of another party at work. Table 9 offers a summary of his conclusions. This table shows that far from enjoying **single-party government**, Britain has experienced a far more complicated situation. If one adds to the table the years between 1950 and 1951, 1964 and 1966, and 1992 and 1997, it may be seen that British politics is not quite as straightforward as some of our politicians and commentators would have us believe. In these periods, politicians have had to partake in the sort of political horse trading so despised of our European neighbours.

Indeed, given the nature of our political parties, it is somewhat disingenuous to describe some of our governments as single-party. Certainly, the experience of Labour in government in the 1970s and of the Major government after 1992 would suggest a single party nominally in power but with internal factions which appear to want to go in different directions.

Table 9: *Periods in British politics when factors/parties other than the governing party played a part in government*		
PERIOD	GOVERNING PARTY	OTHER FACTORS
Jul 1900–Dec 1905	Con	Conservative–Liberal Unionist
Jan 1906–Dec 1910	Lib	Lib majority with Lab and Irish Nat support
Jan 1910–May 1915	Lib	Libs dependent on Irish Nationalists
May 1915–Nov 1922	Coalition	After 1918, coalition dominated by Cons
Jan 1924–Oct 1924	Lab	Lab dependent on Liberals
May 1929–Aug 1931	Lab	Lab dependent upon Liberals
Aug 1931–Sep 1932	Coalition	Government composed of elements of three parties
Sep 1932–May 1940	National	Cons have by far the majority of seats
May 1940–May 1945	Coalition	Genuine coalition despite Con dominance
May 1945–Jul 1945	Con	Caretaker government
Mar 1974–Oct 1974	Lab	Lab dependent upon all other parties not uniting to defeat them
Apr 1974–Mar 1977	Lab	Lab dependent upon all other parties not uniting to defeat them
Mar 1977–Jul 1978	Lab	With agreed Liberal support

SOURCE: ADAPTED FROM BUTLER, 1978, PP 112–13.

THE SIMPLICITY OF THE SYSTEM

It is certainly the case that the British electoral system is easy to understand. In any single constituency contest, the candidate with the most votes cast wins the seat. That candidate becomes the Member of Parliament for the seat and will represent the constituency until the next General Election. It has been argued that the simplicity of the FPTP system is one of its main advantages. Voters are not confronted with lists of candidates for which they should indicate a preference, or complicated quotas which determine how many votes a candidate requires to get elected.

No majority vote for the governing party

It must be stated at this point, however, that while the actual practice of voting and the way in which an MP is elected are very straightforward, problems begin to emerge when all the individual constituency results are added up to arrive at a result for the general election as a whole. Voters are often puzzled as to why a majority of seats in Parliament does not equate to a majority of votes in the country. It may be argued, however, that the explanation is in fact relatively straightforward: if sufficient MPs of the governing party are returned without a majority, then the governing party in Parliament (the sum total of those MPs) will not represent the majority of the electorate.

Geographical seat distribution

The next question which puzzles voters is why, after polling millions of votes as they have done in every election since 1974, have the Liberals (and latterly the Liberal Democrats) received so few MPs? Indeed, in 1983, the Liberal–SDP Alliance polled within two percentage points of the Labour Party and yet returned only a tenth of the seats. Once again there is an answer. It is not as straightforward as the previous one, and it rests on the nature of the distribution of party support across the country. Both Labour and Conservatives have benefited from having support which was fairly well defined in certain locations: Labour doing well in Scotland, Wales and northern England in urban, working class areas, with the Tories generally doing less well in these areas; while the Conservatives have traditionally prospered in the south of England and in suburban and rural areas, with Labour doing much less well in these areas. On the other hand, the Liberals have very few fiefdoms that they can rely upon. What tends to happen is that Liberals do reasonably well in a lot of areas, thus building up a huge number of votes nationally, but do not do sufficiently well in enough constituencies to come first in those constituencies. Hence, between 1970 and 1992, the Liberals/Liberal Democrats have achieved between only 10 and 20 seats. The picture becomes even more confused when looking at other parties. In Chapter 4, we saw how well the Scottish National Party did in the October-1974 General Election, receiving nearly as many seats as the Liberals but with only a fraction of the vote. This is also very confusing to voters. The answer lies in the geographical spread of seats being fought by the SNP compared to the Liberals, with the former contesting only about 70 compared to the 600 or more being fought by the latter.

CONSTITUENCY REPRESENTATION

When considering any alternative to the present voting system, most politicians and pundits point to constituency representation as being of prime importance. It was unrealistic to expect the Jenkins inquiry into electoral reform (mentioned above) to come up with any alternative system which does not include this. Cynics might argue that MPs are bound to raise the notion of constituency representation to almost mythical heights given that it is those same MPs who are performing this function.

MPs' independent judgements

It is clear, however, that even in a system where the accountability of the government ultimately occurs via the MP who represents their constituencies, the bond between the Member and the electors should not be overestimated. The MP, in the tradition of Edmund Burke, is not a mere delegate of the constituents but must exercise judgement which may at times differ markedly from the views of the voters. An MP will, however, listen to what constituents have to say and will attempt to deal with any problem that is brought up at a regular surgery.

However, although, in 1965, the Labour government imported the idea of an *Ombudsman* – an individual charged with dealing with complaints about cases involving public maladministration – it was decided at the time not to allow individuals to approach the Ombudsman direct.

> *One of our big problems was the understandable feelings MPs might have if their constituents were to go straight to the Ombudsman for redress, bypassing traditional parliamentary methods of scrutinising the executive. We provided that all references to the Parliamentary Commissioner* [the official title of the Ombudsman] *should be made through a Member of Parliament.*
>
> Harold Wilson, *The Labour Government 1964–1970: A Personal Record*, Weidenfeld & Nicholson, London, 1971, p 174.

Does the public care?

There is little doubt that the political elite in Britain does consider constituency representation as crucial. A big question does exist, however, over the importance which is attached to the constituency representative by the general public. The weekend surgeries held by the vast majority of MPs are visited by a tiny fraction of constituents, and a worryingly high number of people are hard pressed to actually give the name of their Member of Parliament when asked.

Party power

Very few individuals have been able to hold onto their seats once their party has dispensed with their services. MPs such as Eddie Milne in Blythe was able to hold onto his seat after being deselected by his constituency party in the February-1974 General Election, but his victory was short-lived, for in the October General Election of the same year, he was defeated by the official Labour Party candidate. It would seem that even the most loved constituency representative will eventually succumb to the party juggernaut.

Where individuals seem to be important is not so much as constituency level as at the almost presidential heights of Westminster politics. Since the late 1950s, commentators have suggested an almost gladiatorial contest between the leaders of the major parties in a spectacle which utterly obscures most local issues and most individual candidates. However, although the constituency link should be emphasised as being important, it should not be elevated to such a position that it obscures rational debate about alternative electoral systems.

The following chapters will attempt to address some of the key issues which have arisen in response to the first-past-the-post system, with a view to examining which electoral system might be an appropriate alternative one for Britain.

SUMMARY

The first-past-the-post system is very familiar to citizens of Britain.

It is very easy to understand.

No government in Britain has been elected with over half of the national vote for nearly 70 years.

The system provides for constituency-based representation.

A candidate may win a seat without securing a majority of votes in the constituency.

In the main, governments elected using this system are returned with secure majorities.

Governments tend to be stable and enduring.

Governments tends to be single-party in nature: coalitions are not a familiar feature of British politics.

The system lacks proportionality. Not only does this mean governments lacking a proper mandate, it also results in smaller parties finding it hard to win seats.

Strong government is provided, but at the cost of being unfair to certain political groups.

STUDY GUIDES

Revision Hints

The workings of the first-past-the-post system are very simple. Concentrate on the effects of having such a system.

The implications of the system are very important; especially in respect to MPs representing minority opinion in a constituency and governments representing minority opinion in the country at large.

You should be aware of the circumstances that have made the British electoral system controversial in recent years. Specific instances should be used to back up general statements.

There should be an understanding of the attitudes of the various political parties to the British voting system. Particular emphasis should be put on the changes in attitudes within the political parties.

Exam Hints

- Questions may ask about the strengths and weaknesses of the first-past-the-post system.
- An understanding of the consequences of the British voting system in recent years is essential if one is to fully comprehend what alternative electoral systems do and do not offer.
- An understanding of the concept of the electoral mandate is crucial when considering the first-past-the-post system.
- Questions relating to the wider issues of democracy in Britain will require material learned in this topic.

Practice Questions

1 'The British political system is rendered undemocratic by its electoral system.' Discuss.
2 Outline the main advantages and disadvantages of the first-past-the-post system of voting.
3 How do the main parties differ in their approaches to electoral reform?

9

MAJORITARIAN SYSTEMS

Introduction

THIS CHAPTER WILL look at majoritarian electoral systems. It will consider two such systems: the second ballot and the Alternative Vote, looking, in each case, at how the system works, its strengths and weaknesses, and its suitability for Britain. The case study for the second ballot will look at France, while the case study for the Alternative Vote will look at Australia.

Key points

- The second ballot: how it works; its strengths and weaknesses; its suitability for Britain; case study: France.
- The Alternative Vote: how it works; its strengths and weaknesses; its suitability for Britain; case study: Australia.

The term 'majoritarian' for the purposes of this book, is intended to mean any system of election in which the electorate return a representative with a majority of the votes cast in a particular constituency. Ideally, this system should return a government with at least a majority of the whole electorate, although this doesn't always work in practice. It should be stressed that these systems are *not proportional* and do not produce a distribution of seats proportional to the distribution of votes obtained.

Supporters of **majoritarian systems** claim that the main shortcoming of the simple plurality system (first-past-the-post) is overcome by having a system which returns a representative with over 50 per cent of the votes. Further, it is argued that such a system is likely to be the least traumatic upon our own political system (at least that is what is believed by the proponents of one of the systems described below).

There are a number of majoritarian electoral systems, and there are variations on these themes. For the purposes of brevity and simplicity, this chapter will concentrate on two systems (this will be quite sufficient for examination requirements):

- the second ballot
- the Alternative Vote.

THE SECOND BALLOT

This system is based on the single member constituency, using a **two-ballot system** to ensure that the winner has a majority of the votes cast. A variation of this system is currently used in France, and David Farrell offers a number of other countries which use or have used the system at one of more levels of elections (Farrell, 1997).

As was mentioned at the beginning of this chapter, the purpose of majoritarian electoral systems generally is to secure the election of a candidate with over half of the votes cast. This particular system makes use of two ballots to achieve this result, although the contest may be over after the first ballot.

HOW IT WORKS

In the first ballot, all the votes are counted, and if one of the candidates wins over half of all votes cast, then they are automatically elected. A second ballot only comes into play if no candidate achieves 50 per cent of the vote. This second ballot usually takes place a week after the first. The candidates achieving the most and second-most votes in the first ballot will fight it out head to head in the second, and the winner will be the candidate with the most votes – with the majority of votes cast. There are some variations on the system which enable candidates to proceed to the second ballot, having secured a certain percentage of the votes (see the case study on page 79). In such circumstances more than two candidates could find themselves going forward into the second round. If more than two candidates go into the second round then clearly it is possible for the winner to be elected with less than 50 per cent of the total votes cast.

WHO WINS?

If one candidate is sufficiently popular, then there will be no need for a second ballot and they will be elected there and then. Given that in the 1997 General Election, 47 per cent of MPs were elected with less than half of the vote in their constituencies, it is likely that a significant number of second ballot **run-offs** would take place.

In the second round of voting, electors will have had time to make the decision about who they would like to see elected. This is not a problem for an individual voter if the candidate they voted for in the first ballot goes through to the second. However, if their preferred candidate is eliminated, then the voter has to make a decision based perhaps not on whom they would next like to see elected but instead on those they would definitely *not* like to see elected.

It may well be that the parties themselves will be on hand to provide advice. Perhaps a deal will be struck between two parties that in the event of either of their candidates being eliminated in the first round, they will recommend to their supporters to vote for the other party.

Whatever takes place before the second ballot, the result after the second ballot will be the election of one candidate with over 50 per cent of the constituency vote. However given the unequal size of constituencies and the unequal magnitude of individual candidate majorities, there is no guarantee that the winning party in the assembly will have a majority of seats nationwide.

Indeed, where the system provides for a run-off between more than two candidates, there is a distinct possibility that the overall winner will not have even 50 percent of the constituency votes, which would rather seem to defeat the object of the whole system.

STRENGTHS OF THE SYSTEM

- It provides for candidates to be elected with a majority of votes in the constituency.
- It is easy to understand: voters can easily comprehend the notion of a 'run-off' contest.
- Defenders of this system claim that the two-ballot process gives all candidates a chance early on and enables voters to express a relative choice. According to this view, voting is not about absolutes, and when given the choice, voters would prefer to opt for a candidate nearer to them politically, if their first choice cannot continue.

WEAKNESSES OF THE SYSTEM

- There is a need to prolong the process into two phases, over a week-long period (two weeks in some cases).
- It is a system which asks voters to consider switching allegiances should their preferred candidate in the first round of voting be excluded from the second round.
- There is no guarantee that a governing party, elected using this system will have a majority of votes in the country.

CASE STUDY: FRANCE

In France, the second-ballot system is used both for elections to the National Assembly (lower house) and for electing the President. There is a difference in the mechanisms used for each of these elections however. The rules for electing the President are very much what have been outlined above: a second-round contest between the two front-running candidates in the first ballot. The rules governing elections to the National Assembly are more complex, however, and provide for more than two candidates going through into the second round.

In legislative elections, candidates are able to proceed into the second round of voting if they have obtained a minimum of 12.5 per cent of registered voters (not of actual voters). Clearly, this ruling offers a greater chance to a larger number of candidates than pertains in the election of the President. Whilst it is theoretically possible for up to 8 candidates to go through to the second round (in the extremely unlikely event that there is a 100-per-cent turnout and that all eight obtain exactly the same number of votes), it is more usual for these contests to be between three candidates. In fact, it is unusual for even this to be the case. Godley points out that in French legislative elections in 1993, only 15 such three-way contests took place, and this was out of 450 (representing only 3 per cent) (Godley, 1993).

It is quite possible for the forerunner in the first ballot to lose in the second, due to the shift of support for candidates in the period in between. The most recent presidential elections in France provide a very good illustration of this phenomenon – see Table 10 below. Lionel Jospin, the Socialist Party candidate, topped the poll in the first ballot. Jacques Chirac and Edouard Balladur, however, were from the rightwing Gaullist Party. In the second round, therefore, there was a consolidation of the Gaullist vote around Chirac, who went on to win. The picture was complicated by the far-Right National Front candidate Jean-Marie Le Pen, who urged his supporters to support Jospin in the second ballot.

Table 10: *The result of the 1995 French presidential election*		
CANDIDATE	FIRST ROUND %	SECOND ROUND %
Jospin	22.3	47.4
Chirac	20.8	52.6
Balladur	18.6	
Le Pen	15.0	
Hue	8.6	
Laguiller	5.3	
de Villiers	4.7	
Voynet	3.3	
Cheminade	0.3	

THE SECOND BALLOT: SUITABLE FOR BRITAIN?

Those who would criticise the second ballot from a British perspective argue that the system is totally alien to British voting culture and that the idea of expecting voters to turn up to vote twice in the space of a week would be asking too much. In 1974, there was a six-point reduction in turnout between the two elections in February and October. The conclusion drawn from this observation is that people's interest in politics wanes if there is an over exposure to it in the media, the implication being that two ballots in a week might be too much for voters to take. Certainly, the experience of the 1997 General Election, where the turnout was only 70 per cent even after a full five-year Parliament, is not encouraging in this respect.

The evidence of a fall in voter turnout is mixed, however, when examining the second-ballot system in practice. Farrell indicates that during the 1960s, turnout dropped by over 12 per cent between the first and second ballot (Farrell, 1997). Evidence from the most recent French presidential elections in 1995, however, shows that turnout actually increased between the two ballots. On this basis, it would be difficult to draw any firm conclusions. It may be that the critical factor in voter turnout is not the frequency of ballots, but the interest that is generated among the electorate. In the case of the French presidential election in 1995, the result in the first round was very close for the top three candidates. This might have ignited interest in the second round of voting.

It is true that France changed its voting system in the 1980s, but it may be argued that Francois Mitterand's flirtation with proportional representation in this period was more about keeping the Gaullists out of government than about any obvious dissatisfaction with the two-ballot system.

THE ALTERNATIVE VOTE

Many commentators argue that the Alternative Vote would be the easiest replacement for the first-past-the-post system of election. Historically, it is a system which was recommended by a Royal Commission during the First World War and was almost part of a deal brokered between the Liberals and Ramsay MacDonald in the relatively inactive period of his minority Labour government in 1931. A variant of the system was also the recommendation of the **Plant Report**, which was commissioned by the Labour Party under Neil Kinnock.

HOW IT WORKS

Voters receive a ballot paper (ie a voting form) with the names of the candidates and party affiliation. Unlike any of the systems which we have discussed so far, voters do not simply put a cross against the name of the candidate they want to vote for. Instead, they rank the candidates in order of preference, with their most preferred candidate ranked number one, the second most preferred candidate numbered two and so on until either all the candidates have a number against their names or the voters wish to rank only a certain number of the candidates.

The point of the system (like all majoritarian systems) is to ensure that the successful candidate obtains more than half of the votes cast. When all the votes have been cast and the counting begins, the first task, as is the custom in our present system, is to add up the total number of votes cast. After this has been done, a check is made to find out if any candidate has polled more than 50 per cent. If a candidate has achieved this, then the procedure is complete and the said candidate is duly declared elected to the seat in question.

If, however, no candidate receives over half the total of first-preference votes, the candidate with the fewest first preferences is eliminated from the race and their votes are redistributed to the candidate the voter has marked as second preference. If, after this **redistribution** of votes, one candidate reaches the 50-per-cent-plus-one mark, then that candidate becomes elected, otherwise the candidate who is now last is eliminated from the race and the votes are again redistributed according to second preferences.

Further points

At this point, keen-eyed readers will have spotted a potential problem. Suppose that there are five candidates, say A, B, C, D and E, that no-one polls over 50 per cent and that E, polling the fewest first preferences is eliminated, with second preferences being redistributed to the remaining four candidates. Now suppose, after this redistribution, that still no candidate has reached half and so the next lowest candidate, say D, is eliminated and *their* second-preference votes, in turn, are redistributed. The problem of course is that some of D's first preferences might have voted for E who has already been eliminated and with votes recast. What happens to any such new votes going to E? Clearly, E cannot re-enter the contest as their votes have already been distributed according to the second preferences. Any new redistributed votes to E after D has been eliminated will be redistributed to the three remaining candidates according to the *third* preferences of E's votes.

Another question about this system is what happens to those votes where no preference or maybe only two or three preferences have been expressed. In such cases, the votes cannot be redistributed beyond the number indicated on the ballot paper, after which point they are removed from the counting process.

This process continues, redistributing votes upwards, until one of the remaining candidates has achieved more than half of the total votes.

WHO WINS?

This system will tend to reward the candidate who is the least objectionable to most electors. In a sense, therefore, this system tends to reward the candidate who is the least unpopular rather than the most popular. This hardly seems an ideal recipe for electing a government, in that the incoming administration then has less than a ringing endorsement from the voters. It may be argued, however, that, with the present first-past-the-post system, the scenes of revelry for the victorious party on election night tend to mask the feelings of the majority of voters who certainly in the UK since 1945 have found themselves not voting for the winning party.

The result at constituency level must be distinguished from the result nationally. Although the Alternative Vote provides for candidates to be elected with over half of the support in any single constituency, this does not mean that the government will command the support of over half of the votes nationwide. In Australia in 1954, the Labor Party won over 50 per cent of the national vote but failed to win enough seats to form a government. The reason for this anomaly is due to factors which also prevail in the FPTP system. One party may achieve a large number of seats with narrow majorities, whilst another party may win a smaller number of seats but with much larger majorities. The resulting scenario is that of one party outpolling another, but receiving fewer seats.

STRENGTHS OF THE SYSTEM

- MPs are elected with a majority support of their voting constituents. This is a very powerful justification for this system, particularly in the light of the result of the 1997 UK General Election where more than 47 per cent of British MPs were elected by less than 50 per cent of the votes in their constituents.
- This system is based on single-member constituencies, which would effectively mean that there would be no change to the current arrangement. This would go a long way in assuaging the fears of some that any reform to our system would lead to a break in the bond that exists between MPs and their constituents.
- It is likely to be the most acceptable to the political establishment. The Alternative Vote is closer to the first-past-the-post than other systems, and remains the system which will change the political landscape the least of all.
- This is not a system which is likely to foster the rise of extremist parties. In this respect, it is unlike some of the systems of proportional representation which do enable small parties, often on the far Right or Left, to wield an influence far out of proportion to the support they command in the country as a whole.
- Coalition governments would be no more likely under this system than they are with the current one.

WEAKNESSES OF THE SYSTEM

- The system does not provide for a proportional result. Indeed, **Charter 88** has suggested that the result of the 1997 general Election would have produced an even greater disproportionate result under this system than was actually the case. (Charter 88, 1998).
- Despite each MP being elected by over 50 per cent of the constituency vote, there is no guarantee that the government will have the corresponding support of over half of the national electorate.
- The very fact that many MPs in both Labour and the Conservative Party prefer this system, is an indication that the Alternative Vote is a system which is likely to sustain the current pattern in British politics, with most of its weaknesses and inadequacies.
- The result of this system would be the election of many candidates who were not the first choice of most of the electorate, and this might result in a somewhat lacklustre attitude towards the political process on the part of many voters.
- The system provides no real transfer of power to the electorate: the political parties remain very powerful in being able to select the candidates that are put before the electorate.

THE SUPPLEMENTARY VOTE: VARIATION ON A THEME

In 1991, the Plant Commission reported its findings to the Labour Party. Neil Kinnock had set up this Commission to investigate alternatives to the first-past-the-post system. The report recommended a variation on the Alternative Vote. This system, called the Supplementary Vote, differs from the Alternative Vote in that instead of being able to express preferences all the way through the whole list of candidates on the ballot paper, voters may only express up to two preferences. The second preference is in effect the 'supplementary vote'. Given, however, that Tony Blair asked Lord Jenkins to investigate the array of options once more, Plant's recommendations look to be out of favour at the heart of government.

CASE STUDY: AUSTRALIA

The Australian political system is based on a legislature comprising the Senate (upper house) and the House of Representatives (lower house), both elected directly by the people. The House of Representatives consists of 148 single-member electoral divisions. Elections to this House are based on the Alternative Vote system. The system is based on full **preferential voting**, and a candidate must receive 50-per-cent-plus-one of the votes to be elected. A process of redistribution (as described earlier in the chapter) takes place if no candidate achieves a majority of votes. This process continues until one candidate does secure a majority plus one vote.

Australian electoral law stipulates that voters must express preferences for all candidates on the ballot paper. If a voter only expresses two preferences (as happens in the Supplementary Vote variation outlined above), then the paper is classed as a spoiled one and is declared void.

As with the system in Britain, the largest party in the House will normally form the government. The figures in Table 11, however, show that the result that one might expect from the voting figures does not actually materialise.

Table 11: *Australian election results 1984–1996*			
1984	No. seats	Percentage seats	Percentage votes
Labor	82	55.4	47.5
Liberal	45	30.4	34.4
Nationalist	21	14.1	10.6
AD	0	0	5.5
Other	0	0	2.0
Total seats	148		

1987	No. seats	Percentage seats	Percentage votes
Labor	86	58.1	45.8
Liberal	45	30.4	34.4
Nationalist	21	14.1	10.6
AD	0	0	6.0
Other	0	0	2.3
Total seats	148		

1990	No. seats	Percentage seats	Percentage votes
Labor	78	52.7	39.4
Liberal	55	37.1	34.8
Nationalist	14	9.4	8.4
AD	0	0	11.3
Other	1	0.6	6.1
Total seats	148		

1993	No. SEATS	PERCENTAGE SEATS	PERCENTAGE VOTES
Labor	80	54.4	44.9
Liberal	49	33.3	36.8
Nationalist	16	10.8	7.1
AD	0	0	0.3
Other	2	1.3	10.8
Total seats	148		

1996	No. SEATS	PERCENTAGE SEATS	PERCENTAGE VOTES
Labor	49	55.4	47.5
Liberal	75	30.4	34.4
Nationalist	19	14.1	10.6
Independent and others	5	3.3	14
Total seats	148		

SOURCE: AUSTRALIAN ELECTORAL COMMISSION.

What the figures instead confirm is that the Alternative Vote is an unpredictable system which does not appear to benefit any one party consistently. The Labor Party only really started to benefit from the system in the 1980s after decades of fairly mediocre electoral performances.

During 1980s and 1990s, Labor was able to command majorities in the House of Representatives with much less than 50 per cent of the vote. Indeed, in the election of 1990, for example, it won a majority of seats with only 39.4 per cent of the national vote. Conversely, when Labor lost the election of 1996, the electoral forces were against it in more ways than one. Not only did it find itself out of office, but it also saw that on a vote only fractionally down on the 1990 figure, namely around 39 per cent, it was picking up only 33 per cent of the seats. The party was only 1 per cent behind its Liberal rivals who ended up with over half the seats.

THE ALTERNATIVE VOTE: SUITABLE FOR BRITAIN?

This system has all the disadvantages of a long-time favourite. It has been at the forefront of consideration for replacing the first-past-the-post system for over 80 years, and as such it has been subject to much scrutiny, so much so that the inadequacies of the system are well known, and it perhaps has too many critics for it to gain widespread support for its introduction.

Clearly, this system is not intended to be a proportional one, and so one should not expect the sort of match between votes and seats that is found in a list system for example (see Chapter 10). However, in a system the avowed intention of which is to secure majority rule, the evidence from this brief case study at least suggests that its shortcomings would be a focus of renewed criticism if it were introduced in Britain.

SUMMARY

Majoritarian systems attempt to overcome one of the main problems of the FPTP system, namely the election of candidates with fewer than half of the votes cast in the constituency.

There are two main systems: the second ballot and the Alternative Vote.

Both systems are based on single-member constituencies.

The second ballot requires voters to vote in a second round of voting if no candidate wins a majority in the first.

The second ballot is used in France, where in legislative elections, the system is varied to enable more than two candidates to go through to the second round, thus not guaranteeing a majority victory.

The second ballot does not ensure that governing parties have a majority of the national vote.

The Alternative Vote is used in elections to the Australian lower house and requires voters to express a preference for candidates using numbers 1, 2, 3 etc.

If no candidate is elected with a majority of first preferences, then the lowest scoring candidate is eliminated and their votes are redistributed on the basis of the second preference.

As with the second ballot, the Alternative Vote does not guarantee that the government will have a majority, but unlike the French system, the winning candidate must receive over half of the votes.

The Alternative Vote was a long time favourite to replace the FPTP system and the Plant Commission did recommend a variation of it to the Labour Party in 1991. The Blair government, however, would appear to have thrown open the debate, by the appointment of a commission of its own.

Revision Hints

You should prepare brief summaries of each of the systems outlined in this chapter.

The use of comparative material is valuable. The experience of other countries should be learned in brief.

What do the political parties think of the systems? Remember that the Labour Party looked as if it was going to adopt a variation of the Alternative Vote as its preferred system.

Exam Hints

- Do not confuse majoritarian systems with proportional systems. The former do not result in parties gaining representation in proportion to the number of votes that have been received.
- Do not assume that because MPs are elected with majorities in their constituencies, the government which is formed will have a majority of the votes in the country. The latter does not automatically follow from the former.
- A basic account of how these systems operate may be required. understand the principles underpinning them, and do not get bogged down in their detail.

Practice Questions

1 Outline the main principles and workings of the Alternative Vote.
2 What details of the second ballot might hinder its application in Britain?
3 What is preferential voting? How suitable is such a system for use in Britain?
4 'Majoritarian voting systems are only half an answer in the debate on electoral reform. As such they are not worth considering.' Discuss.

10

PROPORTIONAL SYSTEMS

Introduction

THIS CHAPTER WILL look at proportional electoral systems. It will first discuss how the 1997 British General Election would have turned out under proportional representation, and then point out the varying nature of voter behaviour and proportional systems. It will then go on to examine three such systems: the party-list system; the Single Transferable Vote; and the Additional Member System. In each case, it will look at how the system works, its strengths and weaknesses, and its suitability for Britain. The respective case studies will look at the party-list system used in Israel; the Single Transferable Vote system used in the Republic of Ireland; and the Additional Member System used in the Federal Republic of Germany.

Key points

- The 1997 British General Election: what might have been under proportional representation.
- The varying nature of voter behaviour and proportional systems.
- The party-list system: how it works; its strengths and weaknesses; case study: Israel; its suitability for Britain.
- The Single Transferable Vote: how it works; its strengths and weaknesses; case study: the Republic of Ireland; its suitability for Britain.
- The Additional Member System: how it works; its strengths and weaknesses; case study: the Federal Republic of Germany: its suitability for Britain.

The previous chapter examined two alternative voting systems to the first-past-the-post system (the electoral system currently used in British elections). These systems were not proportional. In other words, political parties would not receive seats in direct proportion to the votes obtained.

Many smaller political parties would still be penalised by the introduction of majoritarian voting systems, despite the fact that there is no guarantee that a governing party will enjoy the support of the majority of the national vote. For these reasons, organisations such as the Electoral Reform Society and Charter 88 have called for the introduction of proportional representation.

WHAT MIGHT HAVE BEEN

If seats in the House of Commons had been distributed in direct proportion to the respective numbers of votes obtained in the 1997 General Election, there would have been no Labour landslide. Indeed, there would have been no Labour majority. Table 12 gives an indication of the actual result, on the one hand, and how things might have been under proportional representation on the other.

Party	% VOTES	SEATS	% SEATS	SEATS WITH PR
Labour	44.4	419	63.6	293
Conservative	31.4	165	25.0	207
Lib Dem	17.2	46	7.0	113
Other	7.0	29	4.4	46

Table 12: *The 1997 General Election in Britain: the actual results and how things might have been under proportional representation*

SOURCE: THE ELECTORAL REFORM SOCIETY.

The Conservatives and the Liberal Democrats significantly underperformed in the election. In the case of the Conservatives, their English vote matched their seats within just a few per cent (33.7 per cent votes to 31.3 per cent seats). In Scotland and Wales, however, the Tories obtained no seats and yet polled just under a fifth in both these countries.

The final column of the table illustrates the outcome of the election had the distribution of seats been identical to the percentage of votes obtained. Labour would have been well short of the 330 seats it would have needed for a bare Parliamentary majority. It becomes clear immediately that coalition government would probably be the result of introducing a form of proportional representation.

In fact, there has not been a single occasion since the 1945 General Election where any party has polled over 50 per cent of the vote. Even in the 1950s, when Labour and the Conservatives between them commanded as much as 96.8 per cent of the vote, the highest either could poll was in 1955, when the Conservatives achieved 49.7 per cent.

THE VARYING NATURE OF VOTER BEHAVIOUR AND PROPORTIONAL SYSTEMS

The difficulty with reading statistics in the above manner is that one cannot simply use the voting figures from one system to extrapolate an outcome in another. In the first place, there is no guarantee that electors would cast their votes in the same way, if a different system were to be used. The second reason – and it is linked to the first – is that there are different types of proportional system available, and they would each give slightly different results.

It may be argued that the above particular statistical exercise is even more problematic. Peter Kellner offers research evidence in which voters taking part in a survey were asked to vote using a variety of proportional methods. In all cases, the Labour majority actually *increased*.

This chapter cannot provide any accurate guide to future voting behaviour: that, as has been seen, depends upon the voters. What can, however, be provided is a guide to the main systems and how each work.

Another important point which should be made is that it is simply not accurate to talk about proportionality as if it were some absolute. The systems which will be examined in this chapter are not equally proportional. This is largely due to the exact manner in which the systems operate, the size of the constituencies and other such factors. The systems may not even display the same degrees of proportionality over time, as social and political forces change absolute and relative voting preferences.

There are hundreds of voting systems in operation around the world, and it would be a pointless exercise in a book of this nature to offer an exhaustive account of them all. Indeed, it is often the case that these systems are variations on a particular theme. What follows, therefore, are three systems which each illustrate the main themes which characterise most of the voting systems used in free, democratic countries:

- the party-list system
- the Single Transferable Vote
- the Additional Member System.

THE PARTY-LIST SYSTEM

This type of system is in widespread use in countries across Europe. There are a number of types of list system, and these became established along with the widening of adult suffrage at the end of the last and the beginning of this century. Many of these systems emerged as it became clear that although majoritarian systems ensured that individual MPs are elected with a majority of the vote in a given constituency, they did nothing to prevent a disproportionate result nationally.

In many ways, this is the most straightforward voting system of all those which are outlined in this book. However, its workings can be very complex, and it will not be possible in a book of this nature to examine all the detailed complexities.

HOW IT WORKS

Instead of voting for a named candidate, voters receive a ballot paper with the names of the political parties on it. Such a ballot paper might look like this:

Mark a cross against the party of your choice	
The Conservative Party	
The Green Party	
The Labour Party	
The Liberal Democratic Party	
The Scottish National Party	

In its simplest form, the votes are added up and the final percentages calculated for each party. If Labour achieved 40 per cent of the vote and there are 659 seats in the House of Commons, that party would be awarded 264 seats. The party would have produced a list of candidates, and in this case the top 264 names on the list would be elected. This system is somewhat novel as it removes any power that the voter has in choosing one candidate in preference for another. In Britain, critics of the first-past-the-post system note a major weakness in the FPTP system as being the lack of voter input into candidate selection. The list system would appear to take this notion to its logical conclusion.

District magnitude

The system outlined above is one of many variations on a theme. It is probably the most proportional of all systems, since here the country is classed as one big constituency, and a very close match may be made between the number of votes cast and the number of seats obtained. This is particularly important for smaller parties who find in smaller constituencies fewer opportunities to build up sufficiently large reserves of votes to enable them to gain representation in a national assembly. The idea of **district magnitude** is thus an important one here.

Regional variations

The **regional variations** to this system enable local lists to be published by the political parties, the aim of which is to provide a greater contact between voters and their elected representatives. The fact remains, however, that with list-based systems, there is no room for the constituency-based MP.

Quota formulae

The simplicity of the system outlined above is somewhat complicated by a variety of methods by which counting can take place. A number of quotas have been devised to ensure the fair representation of smaller political parties. The nature of this book precludes a description of these formulae, but for a fuller discussion on the variety of quotas that may be employed for use with list systems, David Farrell offers a sensible round-up (Farrell, 1997).

WHO WINS?

Parties not candidates

As voters are electing representative not as candidates but from lists provided by the political parties, the question of who wins should really read: which party wins? The successful individuals will probably owe their success more to their loyalty and hard work for their party than to any trust and respect which may have been built up with the local electorate. In this respect, it may be seen that the list-based system is likely to concentrate even more power into the hands of the political parties.

The whole nature of constituency representation is called into question in list systems. This is possibly one of the reasons why it has little support even among pro-reform-minded politicians in Britain. The very idea of abandoning what to many observers is the very cornerstone of our democratic system would be unthinkable.

Regional voting and party variations

The result of an election run on the lines of a list system is likely to be very proportional. This will especially be the case if the country is treated as one large constituency, as happens in Israel (see the case study on pages 94-95). The likelihood of this happening in Britain is also very remote given the regional variations in voting behaviour that are apparent. Scotland and Wales have additional, and in Northern Ireland different, political parties contesting elections. Some form of sub-national or region-based list would be one solution to this problem.

Maintaining proportionality

As mentioned above, one of the problems of decreasing the size of the district will be to reduce the proportionality of the system. One way in which the effects of this may be mitigated is by having a two-tier system of districts. In such a system, the inefficiencies and waste caused at the lower level or tier are compensated at the higher tier level. In practice, this means that parties who might be penalised because of the regional nature of their lists (the Greens, for example, who might not poll sufficient votes in one district to get elected) might obtain representation when all the wasted votes from all the districts are collected at the higher tier.

There is a danger of course of such a system providing an opportunity for small parties with very little support in any one area to nonetheless gain seats in an assembly. Furthermore, there is the danger that such a party, in a finely balanced parliament, would be able to wield an influence far out of proportion to its true level of support. For this reason, most countries using a list-based system operate some level of voting **threshold** above which a party must poll before gaining any seats in an assembly.

STRENGTHS OF THE SYSTEM

- It is very easy for voters to understand (although not necessarily so for the counters).
- It is very proportional: a party receiving 40 per cent of the vote should get 40 per cent of the seats in the assembly.
- Smaller political parties are likely to benefit from having the votes counted as in one large constituency.
- There are safeguards which may be introduced into the system which prevent the disproportionate influence of very small parties.
- There is no need for by-elections in this system. If an MP dies or resigns, the resulting vacancy is filled by the next person on the party list (the list remains in force until the next general election).

WEAKNESSES OF THE SYSTEM

- As the lists are predetermined by the respective political parties, there is even less choice of candidates than exists with the first-past-the-post system. The election in a list-based system empowers the voter to elect a government but not an individual constituency representative.
- As a consequence of the above point, more powers are placed into the hands of party managers. This is likely to lead to a more loyal party but probably more docile and less independent-minded parliamentary party.
- Independent and minority opinion within political parties might be effectively silenced. It may be argued that this would be damaging to an evolving democratic process.
- Given the nature of modern politics and the extreme lengths to which parties go to maximise their vote, it is possible that minorities traditionally excluded from parliament due to insufficient support in any one community will remain debarred.
- There is no direct connection between the voter and the elected representative. As this connection is one of the more cherished aspects of the British political system, it is doubtful that a list-based system would find much favour when reform is being considered.

CASE STUDY: ISRAEL

The Israeli electoral system has been the subject of much debate in recent years. Many commentators have argued that the system has been partly responsible for events unfolding in the Middle East.

Israel operates a list system based upon the country's being one large constituency. Given that Israel has a land area only slightly larger than Wales and a population (approximately 5 million) about the size of Scotland, this arrangement may make a lot more sense than in the UK as a whole which has nearly 60 million inhabitants and a surface area 12 times as large.

The Israeli parliament, the Knesset, has 120 members elected by party list. The main political parties in the country draw up lists of candidates. There is no set way in which the lists are drawn, but the Labour, Likud and Meretz parties all compile their lists through primary elections among registered party members.

An electoral formula, the **D'Hondt Formula**, is used to deal with the issue of 'remaindered votes' since there is never going to be a perfect match between the percentage of votes achieved by a party and the exact amount required for a given number of seats. It is likely, for example, that a party will obtain more than enough votes for say 50 seats but not enough for 51, and the excess (or remaindered) votes over those needed for 50 seats then need to be redistributed.

A quota of 1.5 per cent of the national vote must be achieved before a political party can get any representation in the Knesset. This means that a number of parties might get no seats at all but between them achieve more than 1.5 per cent of the vote. A device exists in this and a number of other list-based systems to enable smaller political parties to link their lists together and hence to benefit from jointly achieving a vote above the threshold. This is called *Apparentement*, and it requires a prior formal agreement between the parties concerned.

The most recent general election in Israel was in 1996 in the aftermath of the assassination of Yitzhak Rabin in November 1995. The two main parties were Labor, with its leader – and Rabin's successor as Prime Minister – Shimon Perez, and the Likud Party, with its leader Benjamin Netanyahu. For the first time, there were separate elections for the position of Prime Minister in addition to elections to the Knesset.

In the presidential race, which was simply a head-to-head between the Prime Minister and his Likud counterpart, Shimon Perez polled 49.6 per cent to Benjamin Netanyahu's 50.3 per cent, and so by a very narrow margin, the Prime Minister was defeated. In order to be able to govern, the Likud Party would need to win enough seats in the Knesset. The final state of the parties was as shown in Table 13.

Table 13: *The results of the 1996 elections to the Knesset in Israel*	
PARTY	SEATS
Labor	34
Likud	32
Shas	10
Meretz	9
National Religious Party	9
Yisrael Ba'aliya	7
Others	19

SOURCE: CNN.

This result suggests a narrow victory for the Labor party, but clearly there is no overall majority (Labor obtaining just over a quarter of the seats). Once all the minor parties had pledged their support to the larger ones, it emerged that Likud could put together a coalition of MPs who were willing to sustain Netanyahu and his administration in office.

BENJAMIN NETANYAHU'S LIKUD PARTY IN ISRAEL NARROWLY GAINED GOVERNMENT IN THE 1996 ELECTIONS TO THE KNESSET – VIA THE PARTY-LIST SYSTEM – AFTER MINORITY-PARTY PLEDGES OF SUPPORT HAD BEEN ACCOUNTED FOR.

THE PARTY LIST: A SUITABLE SYSTEM FOR BRITAIN?

Disproportionality possibility

This system may be seen as coming as close to pure proportional representation as is possible. However, as we have seen, this is not quite the case, as depending on the quota system used in the counting process, some disproportionality may still occur. The system does have attractions, however, which is no doubt why so many countries use one or other type of this system.

The accountability factor

Despite the fact that variations of the list system are by far the most popular voting systems in Europe, it is unlikely that such a system would be attractive in Britain for elections to the House of Commons. Many politicians, academics and journalists would be unable to conceive of a political system in Britain existing without that golden thread of *accountability* which it is believed connects Members of Parliament and their constituents. At election time, MPs are answerable to their local electorate who may choose not to re-elect them if they are unhappy with either their MP's or their MP's party's performance.

Reform measures

The Labour government elected in May 1997, however, is committed to constitutional reform in general and to reforming some (if not all) of our voting practices. Proposals for the Scottish Parliament and the Welsh Assembly are already in place. The government legislated for changes to the way Britain elects its Members of the European Parliament (MEPs). The proposals for European parliamentary elections make provision for the use of a list–based system. The new system will be comprised of 11 super-constituencies in England, each returning a given number of MEPs (the smallest, England North-East, returning 4 MEPs, the largest, England South-East and England North-West, each returning 11 MEPs. London will return 10). Scotland, Wales and Northern Ireland will each be classed as a single constituency, returning 8, 5 and 3 MEPs respectively.

The ballot paper in European elections will contain the names of all the political parties fighting in the 'constituency', as well as the names of any independent candidates who may be standing in the area.

Given that the proposals for the Scottish Parliament and the Welsh Assembly are not the same (see pages 109-110), it would appear that the government is prepared to see a variety of systems in operation side by side at least for the time being.

THE SINGLE TRANSFERABLE VOTE

One of the most striking differences between the party-list system and that of the Single Transferable Vote (STV) is the existence of constituencies. With STV, there is an attempt to combine proportionality with constituency-based representation. One of the main differences between STV on the one hand and the first-past-the-post-system (as well as the second ballot and the Alternative Vote) on the other also concerns constituencies: whereas all the others mentioned are based on single-member constituencies, the Single Transferable Vote uses **multi-member constituencies**.

Once again, the notion of district magnitude comes into play. It would not be possible to provide proportionality in a system solely reliant on representatives elected in single-member constituencies . The district must be large enough, and a number of representatives need to be returned within that district, involving some form of vote redistribution, to enable the result to be proportional.

This system is not widely used. Eire (the Republic of Ireland) uses it for legislative elections. It is also the preferred voting system of the Liberal Democrats and the Electoral Reform Society. Perhaps more significantly, it is actually a system which is used at present in Britain: all local and European elections in Northern Ireland are conducted according to the rules of the Single Transferable Vote.

HOW IT WORKS

Voting is preferential, as with the Alternative Vote: voters express preferences for candidates (1, 2, 3, 4 etc). The aim of the system is more ambitious, however. Instead of simply ensuring a candidate is elected with over half of the vote, the idea is also to ensure proportionality. The workings of the two systems are also similar up to a point: both involve the redistribution of votes, for example. With the STV, however, candidates do not have to obtain 50 per cent plus one vote to be elected (indeed, this would make no sense in a constituency which was electing more than one MP).

The Droop Quota

The number of votes required for a candidate to get elected varies from constituency to constituency depending on the size of the total vote and the number of representatives to be returned. The following **formula**, known as the **Droop Quota**, dictates the number of votes that are needed to get elected in any one constituency:

$$\frac{\text{Number of votes cast}}{\text{Number of seats} + 1} + 1$$

In a hypothetical constituency where 100,000 votes are cast and where there are four seats to be filled, the above formula would be translated as follows:

$$\frac{100,000}{5} + 1 = 20,001$$

In this constituency, therefore, candidates must achieve 20,001 votes to get elected.

Redistribution

If no candidate on the ballot paper achieves the above figure, then, just as with the Alternative Vote, the candidate with the fewest number of first-preference votes is eliminated from the count and their votes are redistributed among the other candidates on the basis of the second preferences expressed. In all likelihood, however, one candidate will probably reach the quota in the first round of counting. Indeed, it is quite possible for a candidate to obtain more than the necessary quota of first preferences, maybe 25,000.

One of the main reasons why the first-past-the-post system is not proportional is that smaller parties may obtain hundreds of thousands of votes nationally but insufficient numbers at constituency level to win any seats. This problem is compounded by successful candidates storing up large majorities of votes way in excess of any requirement to win (perhaps the sole purpose of which is to satisfy feelings of political virility). The Single Transferable Vote aims to deal with both these problems. Once a candidate has reached the required quota to be elected, any votes in excess of the figure are redistributed to other candidates, again according to the second preferences. In the above example, it was suggested that a candidate might obtain 25,000 first preferences (in other words, 4,999 more than the quota requires). In this case, the 4,999 'excess' votes are redistributed to the other candidates.

When redistributing the votes of an eliminated candidate, there is no problem: all the votes are redistributed to the other candidates who have been placed in second place on the eliminated candidates first-preference ballot papers. When redistributing the excess votes of an elected candidate, however, there is a problem. Which votes are redistributed? Remember, only 4,999 of the 25,000 votes are to be redistributed. Which 4,999?

In order to be fair, an idea must be gained of how all of the second preferences were expressed, and then a weighting must be assigned to each vote. In the above example, therefore, all 25,000 votes are looked at and reallocated as fractions. If half of the 25,000 nominate just one other candidate in second preference, then half of the excess votes are allocated to that candidate (half of 4,999 equals 2,499 votes). This is really the only fair way to reallocate the votes.

Whole votes are reallocated from those candidates eliminated from the count (if a candidate fails to reach the quota), and fractions of votes (adding up to the excess votes) are reallocated from those candidates who obtain more than the quota of votes. Many students have difficulty with this process of reallocation at the 'top and tail' of the ballot, and the complexity of the counting process has led many to believe that the system as a whole is unduly complicated. While there is little doubt that the counting process is complex, voters should find the system of voting no more difficult to understand than that of the Alternative Vote.

Candidate numbers

The key difference here, however, is in the number of candidates from each party who appear on the ballot paper. In a constituency which returns four representatives, it is likely that a number of political parties will each put up four candidates. It is likely, therefore, that candidates from the same party will be competing with each other as well as with the opposing parties' candidates for the preferences of the voters. This means that a Labour voter faced with four Labour candidates must choose one to whom to award the first preference, and the others would then presumably appear second, third and fourth on the voter's ballot paper. it could be, however, that one of the Labour candidates is not popular with the voter, in which case the candidate might be placed after a Liberal Democrat candidate or even omitted altogether.

Candidate choice?

Proponents of this system believe it is the only one to offer voters a real say in the election of candidates. Instead of being presented with a *fait accompli* by the political parties (ie one candidate), voters will be able to choose not only between different political parties but also between candidates within political parties. Against this, it could be argued that instead of a *fait accompli* of one candidate, voters will be presented with a *fait accompli* of four or five. After all, the candidates will all have been selected by the party, and in these days of ever-greater-centralisation, there is little evidence to suggest any meaningful choice.

STRENGTHS OF THE SYSTEM

- It maintains the link between the constituent and the elected representative. This increases the accountability of a political system.
- In addition, it ensures that the result of the election will be proportional.
- It gives power to the voters in that they are able to choose from candidates within, as well as between, the political parties.
- This means that voters are able to express their political views more effectively. In preferring one candidate within a party rather than another, the voter is showing support for one wing or body of opinion within the party.
- Constituents would be able to choose from perhaps 5 MPs when it comes to seeking help for a particular problem. It is probable that within any constituency there could be MPs from two or three political parties.

- The government would need to attract the support of over 50 per cent of the national vote. This could lead to coalition government, and supporters of the system would argue that this would provide sensible, consensual politics rather than the adversarial dogfights which have typified the British political system hitherto.

WEAKNESSES OF THE SYSTEM

- It is not as proportional as other systems. This is in the main due to the fact that, in breaking the country down into unlinked constituencies, some compromise of proportionality has had to be made (the notion of district magnitude suggests that the larger the constituency, the more proportional the result).
- Although there is constituency representation in this system, it is not the same as exists in Britain at present. The link would be broken between the constituency and the *individual* MP. The resulting constituencies would be perhaps five times larger than at present.
- It does not empower the voter as much as its defenders would suggest. Ultimately, candidate selection is still in the hands of the party machine. In recent years, the increasing tendency towards centralisation (particularly within the Labour and Conservative parties) is likely to ensure a greater uniformity of candidate: loyal and 'on message' (ie maintaining the party line).
- It is a very complex system, and although the electorate do not need to know the inner workings of the counting process, it may be argued that STV is not sufficiently transparent to ensure that the majority of the electorate are comfortable with it.
- Critics of coalition governments argue that it would create instability and weakness. Although there are times when consensus and agreement is necessary, there are also times when boldness and resolution are required in politics, and the chances of getting these through coalition are remote.

CASE STUDY: THE REPUBLIC OF IRELAND

In the Republic of Ireland, the STV system is used to elect members to the Dail (the Irish Parliament). By law, elections to the Dail must be held every five years, but as in Britain, the Irish Parliament usually has fresh elections before the full term is served. There are a total of 166 members of the Irish Parliament, and they are known as Dail Deputies (TDs). The country is divided up into 39 constituencies, which means that the average number of TDs per constituency is between four and five.

Voters use the preferential system of voting. By casting a vote, 1, 2, 3 etc, the voter is telling the returning officer, 1: A is my preferred choice, but if A does not need my vote or has no chance of being elected, 2: transfer my vote to B; if B does not

need my vote and has no chance of being elected, 3: transfer my vote to C, and so on. The formula to establish the quota is the Droop Quota outlined above (see page 97).

The system is a complex one, although the Irish electorate seem to have developed an instinctive feeling about how to transfer their votes. It must also be said that the counting process is very time-consuming. Indeed, it is usually the evening of the following day before there is some idea of what the new Dail will look like.

The most recent elections to the Dail were in May 1997. A typical result from a constituency is reproduced in Table 14.

Table 14: *The result for the Dublin North constituency in the May-1997 elections to the Dail in the Republic of Ireland*			
Dublin North (4 seats)			
Total number of valid votes	41,158		
Quota	8,232		
CANDIDATE (PARTY)	VOTE	ELECTED 1ST COUNT	ELECTED WITH TRANSFER
Burke R (FF)	8,901	●	
Coyle P (IND)	46		
Daly C (SP)	3,324		
Fallon F (PD)	1,558		
Hyland B (IND)	53		
Jenkinson P (FG)	2,067		
Keaveney A (CS)	686		
O'Brien T (IND)	380		
Owen N (FG)	8,302		●
Ryan A (IND)	715		
Ryan S (LAB)	7,242		
Sargant T (GP)	8,165		●
Wright GV (FF)	8,622		●

The votes refer to the totals after reallocation has taken place. It may also be seen that one of the candidates (Sargant) has been elected with fewer votes than stipulated in the quota (8,165 instead of 8,232). This usually happens when all the votes have been reallocated but vacancies still remain. The system provides for the election of the candidate with the highest number of votes, even if that means the quota is not reached.

After the counting was completed in the 39 constituencies and all 166 Dail Deputies were elected, the state of the parties was as shown in Table 15.

PARTY	SEATS
Table 15: *The number of seats gained by each party in the May-1997 elections to the Dail in the Republic of Ireland*	
Number of seats in Dail: 166 Majority: 83	
Democratic Left	4
Green	2
Fianna Fail	77
Fine Gael	54
Labour	17
Progressive Democrats	4
Sinn Fein	1
Socialist	1
Independents	6
Total	166

The governing Fine Gael–Labour coalition was defeated, with Bertie Ahern's Fianna Fail party only 7 seats short of an overall majority. With the support of independent TDs and Sinn Fien, Ahern's government was approved by 84 to 76 in the Dail.

THE SINGLE TRANSFERABLE VOTE: SUITABLE FOR BRITAIN?

As has been seen, the system is already used for some UK (not British) elections. The question remains: could such a system gain wider support and replace the first-past-the-post system?

Voter – MP link and proportionality
The system does appear to overcome one key criticism of the list system in that the link between the voter and the MP is maintained while at the same time providing a proportional result. On the other hand, it may be argued that the nature of representative government would be transformed out of all recognition and that the traditions of our existing arrangements would be lost forever.

Constituency size and coherence
Furthermore, the size of the constituencies would be necessarily large, perhaps with between 200,000 and 300,000 voters, and this would make the job of

representation very difficult, especially in very sparsely populated regions such as the highlands and islands of Scotland. Furthermore, some constituencies might lack coherence once one has extended out of the urban centres.

Greater flexibility

The system would undoubtedly provide greater flexibility for the voter who could rank candidates both within and between parties in order of preference. It may be argued that voters would simply maintain their tribal loyalties and restrict their choices to a single party. However, there is evidence to suggest that this may not be the case. Dunleavy, Margetts and Weir (1992) have provided survey data which suggests that half of the respondents in one study were willing to express preferences for candidates of more than one party.

Ease of use

It may be further argued that the system overall is too complicated and insufficiently transparent for voters to trust. In response to this, however, it must be said that the Irish electorate appear to be very comfortable with the Single Transferable Vote. Of course, the argument that if it works in one country, then it will work in another is not necessarily a valid one. However, there have been numerous surveys in which voters have been subject to 'mock elections' run on STV rules, and respondents seem to have had few problems with the system.

No widespread use

Perhaps the main weakness of the system is its lack of ubiquity. In short, there are very few countries that use it. Ireland uses it for parliamentary elections, as does Malta. In Australia, it is used for elections to the Senate (upper house). There have been brief flirtations with it elsewhere but these have been short-lived. Political inertia might have been an excuse up to a decade ago, but since the democratic rebirth in the Baltic states and central and eastern Europe, one might have expected a system with so many academic defenders to have been adopted by a number of emerging democracies.

The truth is, apart from a brief interlude in Estonia, no country has adopted the Single Transferable Vote. In such circumstances, and despite such spirited defenders in the Liberal Democrats and the Electoral Reform Society in this country, it is not a favourite for adoption. Indeed, recent government legislation for elections to the Scottish Parliament and Welsh Assembly and to the European Parliament ruled STV out of the reckoning in favour of list-based systems. However, the use of the system in Northern Ireland has been consolidated by the first elections to the new Northern Ireland Assembly.

THE ADDITIONAL MEMBER SYSTEM

This system is really a hybrid: two voting systems which combine to give a proportional result. The name of the system has been criticised, and some would prefer to call it the **two-vote system** because of the way in which this type of voting system has been adopted in some countries. The introductory nature of this book does not permit much time to be devoted to the significance of names. However, the reader may wish to go deeper into this or any of the other systems outlined herein, and the bibliography at the end of this book will offer some guidance.

Perhaps the most prominent user of this system is the Federal Republic of Germany. The case study later in the chapter (see page 106) offers an insight into the workings of the German system. As mentioned earlier, however, the Blair government has used this system for elections to the Scottish Parliament and Welsh Assembly.

Like the Single Transferable Vote, the Additional Member System is able to combine proportionality with constituency representation, and it is therefore often cited as a system which could be adopted in Britain without too much upheaval (see page 109). Unlike STV, however, it does not rely on preferential voting, nor does it involve any complex counting procedure. Some would argue that it retains the best features of the first-past-the-post system while ensuring a high degree of proportionality.

HOW IT WORKS

Two types of vote and MP

There are two key points which characterise this system: first, the voter has two votes to cast – and these votes are cast at the same time; second, two different 'types' of MP are elected to the assembly. The result will be an assembly made up of constituency MPs as well as of a number of others (the so-called additional members), the latter group making the system proportional.

The voter casts one vote for a constituency MP. This process is identical to the first-past-the-post system in that when the counting of the votes takes place, the candidate with most of these votes will be elected, even if they poll fewer than half of the vote.

The second vote is cast for a party; and the voter may wish to vote for a party different from the one supported in the first vote. These votes are then added up to give a national total for each party (it may well be that this total is worked out regionally to take account of regional differences – in which case, the proportionality of the result will be adversely affected to some extent). This second vote is list-based: in other words, it is the parties themselves that determine which of their candidates are elected.

It is the outcome of the second vote that will enable a proportional result to be achieved. The following hypothetical example may help illustrate how the system works.

In this example, the assembly to which representatives are being elected is composed of 100 MPs. The country is broken down into 50 constituencies. Each of these constituencies returns a single member using the first-past-the-post system. The remaining 50 members are elected via the list system according to the party vote cast by electors. Table 16 shows the result of an election involving four political parties. The total number of seats achieved by a party will be based on the percentage of votes it receives through the list vote. This means that some parties (in our example) will have mostly constituency seats with a number of additional members, while other parties which have been unable to muster sufficient support in one constituency will receive most if not all their seats from the list of additional members.

	CONSTITUENCY WINS	% OF PARTY VOTES	ADDITIONAL MEMBERS	TOTAL SEATS
Table 16: *A hypothetical election illustrating the Additional Member System*				
PARTY				
Blue	25	40	15	40
Green	0	5	5	5
Orange	5	20	15	20
Red	20	35	15	35
Total	50	100	50	100

As may be seen from the above result, all the political parties benefit from the additional members, but it gives the greatest help to those smaller parties which fail to win any seats via the first-past-the-post vote: all the votes for these parties have piled up nationally and warrant seats in the assembly.

Minimum threshold

This system may operate with a minimum threshold above which a party must poll in order to gain representation. It may be argued that this is unfair, especially if, as in Germany, the threshold is set quite high (see page 107). On the other hand, it may be argued that if a threshold does not exist or is too low, then extremist parties might be able to wield disproportionate influence as a result.

STRENGTHS OF THE SYSTEM

- The system combines proportionality with constituency representation.
- The constituencies are single-member, so it could be argued that the best of both the first-past-the-post system and the list system is achieved.

- Even if their chosen candidate has no chance of winning, at least voters have a party vote which will go some way to help their chosen party.
- The system has worked well in Germany, countering the critics who argue that proportional systems lead to weak and unstable governments.

WEAKNESSES OF THE SYSTEM

- Half of the MPs elected are not directly accountable to the electorate: they have no effective constituency-based support.
- This means that there will effectively be two types of MP: one with constituency responsibilities (and therefore workload) and one without these duties.
- The list-based element to this system once again gives the political parties a big say as to who will become an MP.
- Some very small parties might find themselves excluded from the assembly despite polling hundreds of thousands of votes nationally.
- Many argue that the system would merely combine the worst aspects of the first-past-the-post system with the worst aspects of the list system: candidates being elected in constituencies with under half of the total vote, and voters having no say over which name appears in which position on the list.

THE BUNDESTAG, THE HOUSE OF ELECTED REPRESENTATIVES IN THE FEDERAL REPUBLIC OF GERMANY, WHERE THE ADDITIONAL MEMBER SYSTEM HAS BEEN USED IN ELECTIONS SINCE 1949.

CASE STUDY: GERMANY

The Additional Member System has been used in elections to the Bundestag, the house of elected representatives in the Federal Republic of Germany, since 1949 when self-government returned to Germany. Since then there have been 14 general elections. Germany is often held up as a model by those who would like to see the proportional electoral system in Britain. For most of the postwar era, Germany has experienced great economic success combined with political stability, and this is an argument to confound critics of proportional representation who claim that it will lead to weak and unstable government.

As in Britain, the government of Germany derives from the governing party in the national assembly. The Bundestag is composed of 656 members who are returned using the dual system of election outlined above. Half are directly elected using the first-past-the-post system in the 328 constituencies, and the other half are elected indirectly by a list-based, proportional system. The lists of candidates are drawn up by the political parties in each *Land* (state).

The proportional result is the one that determines the overall number of seats that the party receives. In other words, a party receiving 40 per cent of the vote will gain sufficient 'additional members' to take the party to that percentage of seats (see again Table 16 above). It may be, however, that a party does so well in constituency seats in the state that it has a greater percentage of the seats than its vote entitles it to have. This is known as **Overhang**. Parties in this situation cannot be denied any of these seats, and so the overall total of Bundestag seats must rise by the size of the 'Overhang'.

A threshold of 5 per cent exists for parties seeking representation via the list. If a party has won three constituency seats, then this threshold is not applicable. The threshold also does not apply to the Danish-speaking 'Suedschlesingshcer Waehlerverband' minority in Schleswig-Holstein because these people have a special exemption. As with the list system of Israel, *Apparentement* is possible whereby smaller parties can formally link their lists so as to maximise their chances of gaining representation. This threshold has led to a sharp reduction in the number of parties being represented in the Bundestag, however: in 1949 there were 12 parties represented, but by 1961 there were only four. It would be over 20 years before the Greens made it five in 1983.

The result of the Bundestag election in September 1998 is represented in Table 17. As may be seen from these results, there is not a perfect correlation between votes and seats (although this is almost impossible to achieve with any truly workable system). The main reasons for this is that the proportional aspect of the system is based on each of the states (the *Länder*) which make up the Federal Republic of Germany. If the list becomes sub-national, then the problem of district magnitude once again rears its head: as the size of the area within which the election takes place decreases, so too does the proportionality of the result.

Table 17: *The result of the September 1998 Bundestag election in the Federal Republic of Germany*

Percentage poll: 47,104,576 valid votes

Turnout: 82.2%

PARTY	% VOTES	NO. SEATS	% SEATS
CDU/CSU	35.1	245	36.6
FDP	6.2	43	6.4
Greens	6.7	47	7.0
PDS	5.2	36	5.4
SPD	40.9	298	44.5

SOURCE: EMBASSY OF THE FEDERAL REPUBLIC OF GERMANY.

FIGURE 15: A SPECIMEN GERMAN BALLOT PAPER

Party-political and economic factors

The German system has come in for some fierce criticism in recent years. This, frankly, has had more to do with the behaviour of the political parties than with the electoral system *per se*. However, many argue that the voting system is instrumental in the problems which have been highlighted.

In the early 1980s, the Social Democratic Party (SPD) (on the Centre-Left of the political spectrum) was in coalition with the 'centre' party, the Free Democratic Party (FDP). In 1982, the FDP decided to walk out of the coalition and join the conservative Christian Democratic Union/Christian Social Union (CDU/CSU). The voters were not consulted, no election took place to determine the change of government which ensued, and the FDP, despite receiving no constituency mandate, has managed to maintain a sufficient (but declining) number of list votes in elections since then.

The FDP has effectively held court in Germany due to its strategic position between the parties of the Left and Right. It could be argued that in a system of proportional representation, this is an almost irresistible position since although support for the FDP is waning, it still retains the role of 'kingmaker' – in other words, that of a party in the Centre which, over time, larger parties are dependent upon. It is this factor which is perhaps worth considering when assessing the Liberal Democrats' advocacy of proportional representation.

The German political system has recently undergone tremendous upheaval after the unification of East and West and the resulting economic problems. It is tempting, therefore, to draw conclusions which tarnish the reputation of the German political system. Nothing could be further from the truth. Germany has enjoyed political stability and unparalleled economic success in Europe. The shortfalls of the Additional Member System there must be seen in the context both of these achievements and of the experiences of other countries using both proportional and non-proportional voting systems.

THE ADDITIONAL MEMBER SYSTEM: SUITABLE FOR BRITAIN?

Optimum system?

This system would appear to allay the fears of many critics of electoral reform in three major respects: it maintains the link between the MP and the constituent; it scores over the Single Transferable Vote in that there is no complicated counting process, and finally there is evidence to suggest that the system can sustain effective government in the long term and that there is not the calamitous instability associated with proportional systems. The fact that the British played a major role in drawing up the system to be used in Germany after the war may provide some insight into the type of system we will one day develop for ourselves.

Earlier in the chapter, mention was made of the voting systems used in the Scottish Parliament and the Welsh Assembly. In both cases, the Additional

Member System is used, although the proportion of list seats to constituency seats is not equal as it is in Germany (for example, in Wales there are 40 constituency seats, based on the 40 Westminster constituencies, and a further 20 list seats).

There are still problems with the system, most notably to do with the party control of the lists and the level of the threshold, which many believe is too high – at 5 per cent in Germany – and is the cause of some disproportionality. No system is going to prove flawless, however, otherwise we would probably be using it already.

A further hybrid

Some critics contend that by maintaining the first-past-the-post system in constituencies, there is still a possibility that an MP could be elected with under half of the constituency vote. Although the national vote would be very largely proportional, a significant number of MPs might be in an assembly under false pretences. This was an issue occupying the minds of some MPs as Lord Jenkins of Hillhead deliberated his findings for his report on reforming the voting system for Westminster elections. Indeed, it has led to another hybrid system to be suggested as a reform, AV+. Depending upon which system one adheres to, AV+ is either a variation of the Alternative Vote or an adaptation of the Additional Member System. The purpose of AV+ is to ensure both a proportional result and that every MP is returned with a majority of their electorate. The system is the same as the Additional Member System except that instead of the constituency vote being based on first-past-the-post, it relies instead on the Alternative Vote. The system would effectively ensure both majority representation in the' constituency and proportional representation in the country.

A future system

The Additional Member System or some variation of it may form the basis of reform of the electoral system in Britain. Of course, those whose criticism against proportional representation is a principled one will never be convinced of the merits of any system other than the first-past-the-post. So while there may be answers to many of the problems associated with reform, a number of questions will inevitably remain. The question which needs to be addressed in these circumstances is whether the problems of any one system of reform outweigh those of the system we have already.

SUMMARY

Proportional representation is not a voting system but a general term covering a number of systems which deliver seats to a party in proportion to the number of votes it receives.

The notion of *district magnitude* will affect the proportionality of a voting system. The larger the area from which the representatives are being elected, the more proportional the result.

A list-based system which treats the whole country as one constituency is likely to provide a more proportional result than one where the list is broken into regions.

The main drawback of the list system is the absence of constituency-based MPs.

Critics of the list system claim that it further enhances the power of the party machine.

Unless some effective threshold exists in a list system, very small parties could find themselves elected and able to wield considerable influence over government.

A list-based system was used in Britain for elections to the European Parliament for the first time in 1999.

The Single Transferable Vote combines proportionality and constituency representation.

Supporters of this system argue that it empowers voters, giving them the right to choose between candidates of the same party.

STV offers citizens more than one MP (perhaps from different parties) from whom they may seek help and advice.

Critics argue that the system lacks transparency and that it is unduly complicated.

Some constituencies would by necessity be very large and difficult for MPs to maintain effective links with.

STV operates for elections in Northern Ireland other than those to Westminster (ie STV is used to elect councillors and MEPs).

The Additional Member System is claimed to offer the best of all worlds: a proportional system, with constituency representation, and a system which people will find easy to understand.

Critics, on the other hand, argue that it offers the worst of all worlds: the list element of the system keeps the party leaderships firmly in control, and the first-past-the-post part of the system will enable many MPs to be elected without the approval of the majority of their constituents.

The system has worked well in Germany since 1949. Despite critics' fears about PR, Germany has maintained a stable political system and a strong economy for much of this time.

AMS was used to elect members of the Scottish Parliament and the Welsh Assembly in the first such elections in 1999.

Revision Hints

One of the key concepts to understand is that of *district magnitude*. The larger the constituency, the greater the potential there is for a proportional result.

You should have a grounding in the basics of each system of proportional representation.

Examine the impact of different systems of proportional representation and how they work in different countries. Remember that comparative analysis is an assessed element of the core module in A Level syllabuses.

You should be able to compare and contrast proportional systems with each other as well as with the first-past-the-post system.

Exam Hints

- Questions may focus on the strengths and weaknesses of proportional representation generally and/or systems in particular.
- Examine the attitudes of the main political parties on the question of proportional voting systems. To what extent have these attitudes changed?
- Have there been any recent, significant developments to the debate on electoral reform generally and proportional representation in particular?
- What are the prospects for change?
- What impact might these changes have on the political system in Britain?

Practice Questions

1 Outline the circumstances through which the issue of proportional representation came onto the political agenda.
2 'Proportional representation does not equal proportional power.' Discuss.
3 Identify and explain two systems of proportional representation. Which one would be most suited for adoption in Britain?
4 Describe and account for the changing climate of opinion about the introduction of proportional representation in Britain.

11

CONCLUSION

THIS CHAPTER WILL give a summary of what has been discussed in this book, looking first at voting behaviour in Britain from 1950: the era of alignment, the era of uncertainties; then at the electoral systems covered: first-past-the-post; majoritarian systems: the second ballot, the Alternative Vote; proportional systems: the party-list system, the Single Transferable Vote, the Additional Member System; and finally at the issue of electoral reform in Britain.

Key points
- Voting behaviour in Britain from 1950: the era of alignment; the era of uncertainties.
- Electoral systems: first-past-the-post; majoritarian systems: the second ballot, the Alternative Vote; proportional systems: the party-list system; the Single Transferable Vote, the Additional Member System.
- Electoral reform in Britain.

VOTING BEHAVIOUR IN BRITAIN FROM 1950

In the first part of this book, an attempt was made to examine the nature of voting behaviour in Britain in the years from 1950 onwards. The period may be divided as follows.

ERA OF ALIGNMENT

First was an era characterised by political stability where two political parties dominated the political arena and third parties only rarely made an impact on the system. The main determinants of voting behaviour were based upon alignments of social class and party identification. These alignments, however, were not perfect fits and they did not preclude political dynamism: in other words, there were changes of government. However, these latter tended to be based on only modest swings of political support.

ERA OF UNCERTAINTIES

After 1970, it would appear that many of the certainties of the earlier period weakened (though they did not disappear). Some of the forces at work here had their roots before 1970, but it was after this date that the changes become manifest. The once-impregnable two-party fortress was breached, and its combined share of the vote declined significantly. The main causes of these changes appeared to be the decline in the strength of partisanship and a weakening of the links between social class and party political support.

In spite of these shifts of support away from the two main political parties, other political groups were unable to make the political inroads that one might have expected. Labour had to limp on in office for five years after the elections of 1974, and the Conservatives enjoyed a dominance in British politics for 18 years after 1979. True, the Scottish National Party was able to make a big impact north of the border in the 1970s, but for third parties, fielding candidates nationwide and amassing millions of votes, there was little reward in terms of seats. The nature of the electoral system came in for particular criticism from this time, and despite (and maybe because of) large government majorities since then, the issue has not gone away.

Clearly, the Liberal Democrats, who have much to gain from the reform of the electoral system, have been dogged in their criticism of the first-past-the-post voting system. Other groups, such as the Electoral Reform Society and Charter 88, have added their voices in the campaign for fair votes.

ELECTORAL SYSTEMS

In examining the alternatives to the first-past-the-post system, the second part of this book considered a number of themes. As well as explaining both the workings of the systems and their main advantages and disadvantages, a number of questions were asked: how do the systems work in other countries? Would they be suitable for use in Britain?

The first-past-the-post system could be maintained because it is easy to understand, it maintains the political status quo and it seems to result in the election of governments that remain in power long enough to enact at least some of their manifestos. The downside of this of course is that each such **manifesto** is being enacted without a proper electoral mandate. No government since the National Government of 1931 has been elected with a majority of the votes.

MAJORITARIAN SYSTEMS

Majoritarian systems have attempted to overcome the problem of MPs elected without a majority of votes. The second ballot effectively operates by a process of elimination. If no candidate receives a majority of votes in the first ballot, then a second is held between the top two candidates. The Alternative Vote achieves a similar result using one ballot, but in this case, voters express their preferences for different candidates. If no candidate gets over half of the first-preference votes, the candidate with the fewest is eliminated and those votes are redistributed to the remaining candidates. This continues until one candidate is elected with over 50 per cent of the votes. The problem with both these systems is that they do not ensure that the government is elected with 50 per cent of the vote, and as such they are not systems that are supported by those who prefer proportional systems.

PROPORTIONAL SYSTEMS

Proportional representation is not a system as such but a term to cover systems which do result in a proportional relationship between the number of votes obtained by a party and the number of seats it receives in the assembly. The party-list system simply involves candidates' choosing a party. The total vote for any party will determine the number of seats it receives, and MPs are then allocated from the various party lists. The problem with this system is that it effectively severs the link between the MP and the constituent. The Single Transferable Vote overcomes this problem by having multi-member constituencies where voters express a preference for the different candidates. To be elected, candidates must reach a quota, and votes in excess of this quota are reallocated to other candidates. If no candidate reaches the quota, then the lowest-placed candidate is eliminated and the votes are reallocated (as with the Alternative Vote). Although this system is preferred by the Liberal Democrats, many criticise it for its complexity and the size of its constituencies.

The German voting system, the Additional Member System, is a hybrid, a combination of the first-past-the-post system and the party list. Proportionality is achieved here by additional members from the list being combined with the FPTP winners in the constituencies. This system has attracted criticism because it creates a two-tier system of MPs: one tier which represents constituencies, and another one which has no constituency link, thus having a less direct line of accountability.

ELECTORAL REFORM

Ten years ago, the debate about electoral reform would have been wide open. Which system to employ was no more than an academic question. There was little prospect of seeing a government elected which would enact such constitutional change. The Blair government, however, has already made changes which may even extend to the election of MPs to the House of Commons.

- Elections to the European Parliament are based on the party-list system. Scotland, Wales and Northern Ireland will be classed as one constituency each, with England having 11 super-constituencies. Each of these constituencies has its own party lists.
- Elections to the Scottish Parliament and the Welsh Assembly are by a variation of the Additional Member System. There are 40 Assembly constituency seats in Wales (with the same boundaries as for the House of Commons) with a further 20 additional members (Scotland has a similar ratio).

In the past, one might have been forgiven for cynically observing that these changes make little difference between the main focuses of power in Britain. Once again, however, the government has surprised many by opening out the debate to include Westminster elections as well. Clearly, there is talk of electing members to the second chamber, but also of changes to the way we elect MPs.

Lord Jenkins of Hillhead, a Liberal Democrat Peer but also a former Labour Cabinet minister, was (as already mentioned) asked by Tony Blair to investigate the alternatives and come up with a series of recommendations. Proposals will eventually be put to the people in a referendum.

Once again, the cynically-minded might observe that the public has little appetite for such constitutional matters. Indeed, the issue of the voting system never appears at the top of lists of issues when opinion-poll results are published. Could it be that the entire exercise is little more than an attempt to satisfy reformers such as Robin Cook, or to buy off the chattering classes who really do seem to care about the issue?

The fact remains, however, that at the beginning of the twenty-first century, the only elections to be held using our current voting system will be those which return MPs to the House of Commons, and local elections. In previous years, there would have been the excuse that the first-past-the-post system was used in most UK elections. Soon, however, there may be a momentum for change that it might not be possible to resist. Voters will be used to using two, three or – in the case of Northern Ireland – four different systems. There will no longer be the fear of the unknown. Whatever the outcome, the political upheavals of the past generation have played their part in bringing Britain to the brink of a new constitutional age.

GLOSSARY

Affluence   In the context of this book, affluence refers to the increasing prosperity of individuals. Some commentators have suggested that there may be a causal link between rising standards of living and voting behaviour.

Alford Index   A way of measuring class voting. The calculation works for either Labour or the Conservatives. For Labour, deduct the party's percentage share of non-manual workers from its share of manual workers (the range is 0–100; in other words, if all Labour voters were manual workers, then the calculation would be $100 - 0 = 100$).

Apparentement   The provision of a list-based system where parties (usually smaller ones) may link their lists for the purposes of seat allocation. This maximises their chances of getting some representation between them.

By-election   In Britain, an election which takes place in a constituency where a vacancy has arisen due to either the death, resignation or disqualification of a Member of Parliament.

Charter 88   An organisation at the forefront of campaigns to secure constitutional reform in Britain.

Class alignment   The theory which attempts to link social class to party political support. It has been observed that during the 1950s and 1960s, a clear majority of working-class people supported the Labour Party, with an overwhelming proportion of the middle-class supporting the Conservatives.

Class dealignment   The theory that from the 1970s onwards, the link between social class and vote becomes weaker, to the extent that by the 1980s, more working-class people were supporting the Conservatives.

Coalition government   Where a political party falls so short of a parliamentary majority that it may be necessary for it to seek a partnership with another party or parties to form a coalition government. This is not the norm in British politics. In countries operating proportional voting systems, however, they are quite common.

Constituency   The geographical district used in elections. Depending on the electoral system used, these districts may vary both in size and in the number of representatives to be returned in each.

Constituency representation   Where MPs are returned from geographically defined areas. Voters in those areas therefore have a named individual to whom they may take their problems.

Cross-class location   Where an individual or family display characteristics from more than one social class. A husband and wife may not both have occupations of the same social class. Or again, a working-class family might own its own home.

Cube Law   During the 1950s and early 1960s, elections were won on relatively small shifts in votes. A relationship was observed where for every percentage-point shift in votes there was an accompanying percentage shift cubed in seats.

D'Hondt Formula   The formula which is used for most list-based systems. It is used in the counting of votes in elections in Israel, for example, where a party's remaindered (or excess) votes are redistributed.

Deferential voters   Those who support a political party mainly in the belief that the leaders of that party are in some way their betters. It is most commonly applied to working-class voters supporting the Conservative Party in the 1950s and 1960s.

Deviant voters   Voters who do not support their natural party of class – for example, working-class Conservatives and middle-class Labour supporters.

District magnitude   That which relates to the size of the electoral area, which is related in turn to the number of representatives to be elected. Normally, the larger the district magnitude, the more proportional the result is likely to be.

Dominant-party system   Where one party dominates the political agenda over a long period of time. Other parties then experience long periods of opposition. It may be argued that Britain had a system dominated by the Conservatives between 1979 and 1997.

Droop Quota   The formula which determines the number of votes required to win a seat in the Single Transferable Vote. The total number of votes cast is divided by the number of seats to be allocated, plus one. The total is then plussed by one.

Embourgoisement   The theory that as members of the working class became more affluent, they would behave more like the middle class and vote Conservative.

Filter model   In a strongly aligned period, it has been argued that voters effectively screen out media messages which appear not to concur with their own party support. The impact of the messages is blunted for a significant proportion of the population.

Floating voters   Those individuals who do not have strong ties to a political party. They are most prone to switching their support from one party to another. It is this group of voters that parties have traditionally targeted since they are more likely to be swayed by political messages.

Formula   Essentially, the calculation that is employed for counting votes and allocating seats.

Franchise   The right to vote in elections. The word is also often used to indicate the number of people who are able to vote.

Gerrymandering   A term to denote the deliberate drawing of constituency boundaries in such a way as to benefit one party or group.

Ideological disjuncture   Where a rift appears to have developed between a party and its traditional supporters, usually characterised by disaffection of voters with the core policies of the party. It has been suggested that this was a reason why the Labour Party did so badly in elections in the 1980s.

Landslide   When one political party wins a very large majority of seats in the House of Commons.

Majoritarian system   An electoral system the aim of which is to ensure that MPs are supported by at least half of their constituents. The systems do not guarantee that a government is elected with at least 50 per cent of the voters. The best known of these systems are the second ballot and the Alternative Vote.

Majority government   Government by a party that commands a majority of seats in an assembly.

Mandate   The authority given to a government to carry out its electoral promises. Some controversy exists about whether a party has a proper mandate if it has failed to poll at least 50 per cent of the vote.

Manifesto   The programme of policies set out by a party in a general election. If the party is elected, the promises made in the manifesto will become the basis for the government's legislative programme.

Minority government   Where a party seeks to govern without a majority of seats and does not enter into a coalition with another party. In such circumstances, the government is vulnerable to defeat in votes in the House of Commons. Between February and October 1974 and between 1976 and 1979, Britain had a minority Labour government.

Multi-member constituency   Where voters are electing more than one Member of Parliament to represent their constituency. The Single Transferable Vote is a system where these are found.

Overhang   In Germany, using the Additional Member System, a party may do so well in the constituencies that it may end up with a higher percentage of seats than votes. The party is allowed to keep those extra setas, and the overall size of the Bundestag is increased until the next election.

Partisan alignment   Also known as party identification. A psychological attachment to a political party, which may vary in strength. It is more than simply voting for a party: it is argued that the 1950s and 1960s, partisan alignment was one of the anchors of the stable two-party system.

Partisan dealignment   It has been suggested that the strength of partisanship has weakened, and as a result loosened the attachments that individulas have to political parties.

Plant Report   A report on electoral reform commissioned by the Labour Party. Professor Raymond (now Lord) Plant of Southampton University was asked to investigate alternatives to the first-past-the-post voting system. The final report was published in 1991.

Preferential voting   Rather than placing an X on the ballot paper, voters here are asked to express their vote in preferential terms (1, 2, 3, 4 etc). The Alternative Vote and the Single Transferable Vote are examples of preferential voting.

Press deficit   This refers to the gap which exists between press support for the Conservatives and that for Labour. Traditionally, most newspapers have supported the Conservatives. Labour has never won when the gap has been more than 18 per cent.

Proportional representation   Not a system of voting but a collective term used to describe an electoral system in which the proportion of seats that a party obtains in an assembly matches the percentage of votes that that party receives.

Psephology   A commonly used word which has grown up over recent decades. It refers to the study of elections and voting behaviour.

Quota   The figure, used in election counts, which determines the number of votes required to win a seat.

Rational voting   Where voters carefully evaluate all sides of an argument or issue before casting their vote.

Realignment   After political dealignment, where old certainties begin to weaken and no longer hold true, there may be the building of a new political order to take its place. After the decline of the old Conservative–Liberal alignment of the late nineteenth and the early twentieth century, a new alignment gradually emerged based on the dominance of Labour and the Conservatives.

Recall data   Statistics based upon asking respondents to cast their minds back and remember how they cast their vote five years ago, for example.

Redistribution   In a preferential voting system, votes may be reallocated if, for example, no candidate has achieved the **quota** necessary to be elected. Votes in excess of the quota may also be redistributed to other candidates. The Alternative Vote and the Single Transferable Vote usually involve the redistribution of votes.

Referendum   Where a vote is taken on a question put to the people of a country. In Britain, there has only been one nationwide referenduum, namely in 1975 on whether it should have remained part of the European Economic Community. There have also, however, been referendums in Scotland and Wales over the issue of devolution.

Regional variations   This usually refers to differing levels of support for political parties, varying from one region to another. After 1979, a North–South divide appeared to open up. Labour did markedly worse in elections the further south one went. Indeed, in 1983, south of a line from the Wash to the Bristol Channel (excluding Greater London), Labour was virtually wiped out in terms of MPs. This trend appeared to be reversed somewhat in 1992, with the Conservatives making gains in Scotland. Of course, in 1997, Labour made major inroads into the Conservative heartlands of southern England.

Reinforcement   Traditionally, it was considered that the media had a reinforcing effect upon people's political attitudes, especially during the period of aligned voting. Recent evidence suggests that perhaps the media may actually influence attitudes.

Run-off   In the second ballot system, if no candidate wins over half of the vote in the first round, the top two candidates are involved in a second vote where one will win.

Salariat   In the Heath, Jowell and Curtice reassessment of the dealignment thesis, there was an attempt to reclassify the occupational structure. This new classificiation brought together managers, administrators, supervisors of non-manual workers, professionals and semi-professionals.

Sectoral cleavages   The idea that the old cleavage or division in society based on occupation (or social class) has been replaced by a new division between those who work and consume in the public sector and those who work and consume in the private sector. Clearly, it is unlikely that there are many who fit this division 100 per cent, but it is argued that a public-sector worker living in a council house is more likely to support the Labour Party than is a private-sector worker who is an owner-occupier.

Secret ballot   Here, voters are able to express their political preference in a manner which protects them from intimidation. In fact, in Britain, the vote is not technically secret. All ballot papers are coded and counterfoiled to enable officials to deal with any later breaches of electoral law which may arise.

Selected retention   The filter model, outlined above, suggests that in the past voters were able to screen out messages which did not concur with their own effectively by remembering only those messages with which they were in agreement.

Simple majority system   Another name for the first-past-the-post system.

Single-member constituency   Quite simply, where voters are electing only one Member of Parliament to represent their constituency.

Single-party government Where one party is able to form a government without the need to approach another party in order to form a coalition.

Social class A classification which is usually based upon occupation. Broadly speaking, 'working class' refers to manual workers, and non-manual workers are normally referred to as 'middle class'.

Swing The shift in votes between the political parties from one election to the next. Usually expressed in percentage terms.

Target seats In an election, political parties are able to identify the seats they believe they stand the greatest chance of gaining from another party. These seats are treated as priorities, having more campaign resources and big names devoted to them.

Threshold In proportional systems, this is the minimum percentage vote that a party must achieve before being able to gain representation. In the German Bundestag, it is 5 per cent.

Two-ballot system Another name for the second ballot system.

Two-party system Where two parties appear to dominate the political system. It has been argued in Chapter 2 that Britain had a two-party system in the 1950s and 1960s. This argument is not without its critics, however.

Two-vote system This normally applies to the Additional Member System where voters cast two votes (albeit usually on the same ballot paper).

Volatility It may be argued that after the political stability of the 1950s and 1960s, the British political system became more volatile. There appeared to be large shifts in votes in 1979, and large shifts in seats in both 1983 and 1997. The evidence for electoral instability, however, lacks consistency.

FURTHER READING

The following titles provide a good follow-up to this book. They will expand and develop themes as well as introduce points which could not be raised here.

Butler, D. (1995) *British General Elections Since 1945*, Oxford: Blackwell. A wide-ranging book with some good historical context.

Denver, D. (1994) *Election and Voting Behaviour in Britain*, London: Prentice Hall/ Harvester Wheatsheaf. An excellent, detailed book. A must for teachers.

Denver, D. (1997) 'The 1997 General Election Results: Lessons for Teachers' in *Talking Politics*, Vol. 10, No. 1 Autumn 1997, pp. 2–8.

Dunleavy, P. (1980) 'The political implications of sectoral cleavages and the growth of state employment' in *Political Studies*, Vol. 28, Nos 3 & 4, pp. 364–383 and 527–549. For readers wishing to find out more about the sectoral-cleavages thesis.

Dunleavy, P., Margetts, H. and Weir, S. (1992) 'Replaying the 1992 General Election: How Britain Would Have Voted Under Alternative Electoral Systems', LSE Public Policy Paper, Number 3. An interesting 'What if?' analysis.

Farrell, D. (1997) *Comparing Electoral Systems*, London: Prentice Hall/Harvester Wheatsheaf. A very good, detailed survey of different electoral systems and where they operate, an ideal next step from this book.

Heath, A., Jowell, R. and Curtice, J. (1985) *How Britain Votes*, Oxford: Pergamon. An attempt to re-evaluate the dealignment thesis.

Linton, M. (1995) 'Sun Powered Politics' in *The Guardian* (Media), 30 October 1995. A good examination of the impact of the tabloid press in the 1992 General Election.

Miller, W. (1991) *Media and Voters: The Audience, Contents and Influence of Press and Television at the 1987 General Election*, Oxford: Clarendon Press.

Norris, P. (1997) *Electoral Change Since 1945*, Oxford: Blackwell. A very useful book for both context setting and contemporary analysis.

Other useful books, which are more specialised and perhaps more suited to teachers:

Bogdanor, V. and Butler, D. (1983) *Democracy and Elections: Electoral Systems and Their Political Consequences*, Cambridge: Cambridge University Press. This book provides a useful guide to the workings of various electoral systems from around the world. Although quite an old book, many of the principles therein remain valid today.

Butler, D. (ed) (1978) *Coalitions in British Politics*, London: Macmillan.

INDEX

Butler, D. and Butler, G. (1994) *British Political Facts 1900–1994*, London: Macmillan. A mine of political information.

Butler, D. and Stokes, D. (1974) *Political Change in Britain*, London: Macmillan Press.

Campbell, A., Converse, P., Miller, W. and Stokes, D. (1960) *The American Voter*, New York: John Wiley & Sons, Inc.

Crewe, I. (1986) 'On the death and resurrection of class voting: some comments on How Britain Votes' in *Political Studies*, Vol. 35, No. 4, 1986, pp. 620–638. A critique of the Heath, Jowell and Curtice book.

Crewe, I. (1992) 'Partisan dealignment ten years on' in Denver, D. and Hands, G. (eds) *Issues and Controversies in British Electoral Behaviour*, London: Prentice Hall/Harvester Wheatsheaf, Chapter 4.2, pp. 141–147.

Crewe, I. and Denver, D. (1985) *Electoral Change in Western Democracies*, London: Croom Helm, p 139.

Crewe, I., Sarlvik, B. and Alt, J. (1977) 'Partisan dealignment in Britain 1964–1974' in *British Journal of Political Science*, Vol. 7, No. 2, 1977, pp. 129–90. This was one of the pioneering pieces of work which developed the partisan dealignment thesis.

Curtice, J. and Smetko, H. (1994) 'The impact of the media' in Heath, A. *et al.* *Labour's Last Chance?* Aldershot: Dartmouth.

Denver, D. and Hands, G. (1992) *Issues and Controversies in British Electoral Behaviour*, London: Prentice Hall/Harvester Wheatsheaf. An in-depth piece of work which teachers might find useful.

Dummet, M. (1997) *Principles of Electoral Reform*, Oxford: Oxford University Press.

Godley, D. B. (1993) 'The French General Election of 21–28 March 1993' in *Electoral Studies*, Vol. 12, pp 291–314. Perhaps too detailed for the core module at A Level, and more appropriate for students taking the comparative paper.

Nordlinger, E. (1967) *Working Class Tories*, London: Macgibbon & Kee.

Pulzer, P. (1975) *Political Representation and Elections in Britain*, London: George Allen and Unwin Ltd.

McKenzie, R. and Silver, A. (1968) *Angels in Marble*, London: Heinemann. The classic work on working-class Conservatism.

Sarlvik, B. and Crewe, I. (1983) *Decade of Dealignment*, Cambridge: Cambridge University Press.

Trenamen, J. and McQuail, D. (1961) *Television and the Political Image*, London: Methuen.